S0-BAI-849

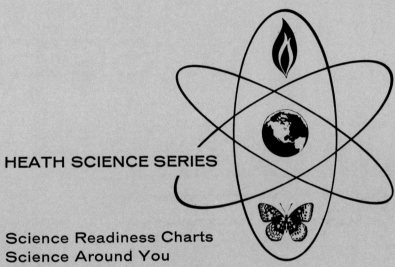

HEATH SCIENCE SERIES

3 SCIENCE

Far and Near

THIRD EDITION

By Herman and Nina Schneider

D. C. Heath and Company Boston

Illustrations by WALTER SKOR
JAMES GORDON IRVING
WALTER FERGUSON
and Alex Ebel
Louis Cary
Cheslie D'Andrea
George Parrish
Cover design by Frank Fretz

Printed January, 1967

Copyright © 1965 by D. C. Heath and Company
Printed in the U.S.A.

D. C. HEATH AND COMPANY
Boston, Englewood, Chicago, San Francisco,
Atlanta, Dallas, London, Toronto

CONTENTS

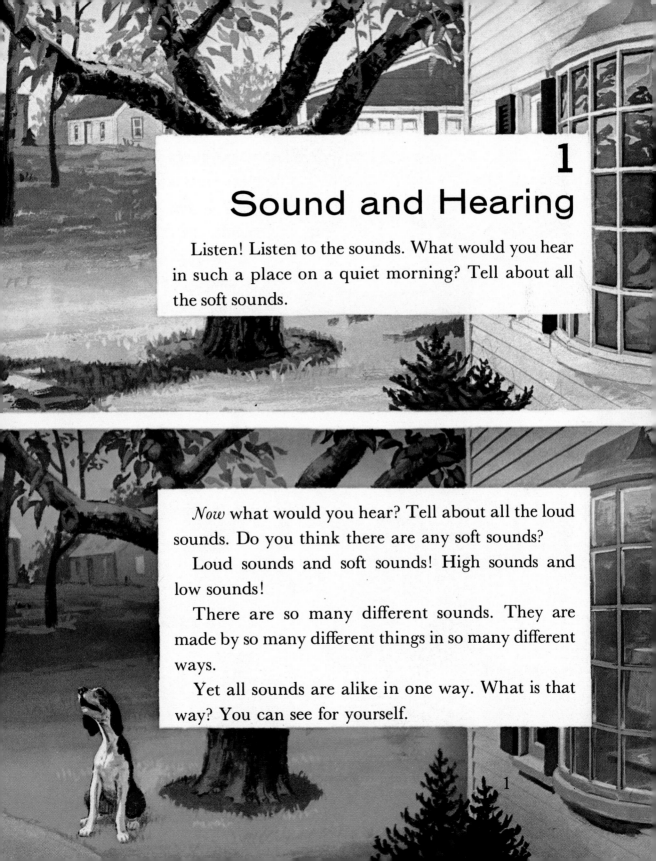

1
Sound and Hearing

Listen! Listen to the sounds. What would you hear in such a place on a quiet morning? Tell about all the soft sounds.

Now what would you hear? Tell about all the loud sounds. Do you think there are any soft sounds?

Loud sounds and soft sounds! High sounds and low sounds!

There are so many different sounds. They are made by so many different things in so many different ways.

Yet all sounds are alike in one way. What is that way? You can see for yourself.

EXPERIMENT

You will need some dry cereal and a toy drum.

Put a few grains of dry cereal on the middle of the drum. Then strike the drum near the edge. What happens to the cereal? What makes it move?

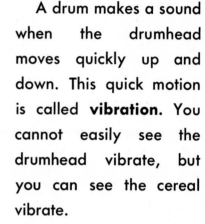

A drum makes a sound when the drumhead moves quickly up and down. This quick motion is called **vibration**. You cannot easily see the drumhead vibrate, but you can see the cereal vibrate.

Do the experiment again. This time hold one hand down on the drumhead when you hit it.

Does the drum vibrate as much?

Is the sound as loud?

Do other sound-makers vibrate when they make sounds? You can find out.

2

TRY THIS

You will need some dry cereal, thread, and toy sound-makers.

Tie a thread to a grain of cereal. Hold it like this, near a sound-maker. Then pluck the strings. What happens?

Try other sound-makers. To make sound, each one of them must vibrate.

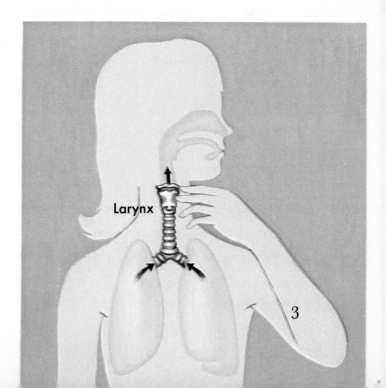

You Make Sound

What vibrates when you make a sound?

Hold your fingers like this and buzz like a bee. Can you feel the vibration from your own sound-maker?

Inside your throat is your voice box, or **larynx.** When you speak, your breath passes through the larynx. Your breath causes parts of the larynx to vibrate.

Larynx

3

Sound Conductors

A jet plane flies overhead. It is far away, but you can hear it.

A friend calls to you. He is across the street, but you hear him.

The sound vibrations get from one place to another through the air. We say that air conducts sound. To *conduct* means "to lead." Here is a way to show that air conducts sound.

EXPERIMENT

You will need a sheet of paper, a handkerchief, and a watch.

1. Roll the paper into a tube. Hold the watch at one end. Put your ear to the other end. Do you hear the watch ticking?

What is inside the paper tube? Nothing but air. Does air conduct sound?

These two space travelers are planning a trip to the moon. They know that there is no air on the moon. They know, and you know, that sound travels through the air. How will they talk to each other when they get to the moon?

Does sound travel through other substances as well as through air? Try part 2 of your experiment.

2. Open the paper tube and put a rolled-up handkerchief in the middle. Seal the tube. Repeat the test as pictured on page 4. Now can you hear the ticking of the watch? Do you think cotton conducts sounds as well as air does?

Is there a better way to conduct sound? Let's find out.

EXPERIMENT

You will need a plastic ruler, a wooden ruler, a piece of cotton, a piece of sponge rubber, a handkerchief, a large nail, and a pencil. Have someone help you.

Put your head down, with one ear pressed against the table. Cover your other ear. Let your helper tap one end of the wooden ruler. The other end is pressed against the table. Does sound travel through the wooden ruler and through the table?

Now lift your head and listen to the sound. It is coming to you through the air. Which way is louder? Which conducts sound better, air or wood?

Now try the plastic ruler. Does sound travel through hard plastic?

Now try it with the cotton as pictured above. Try other soft and hard things. Does sound seem to travel better through soft materials or hard materials?

Could the space travelers talk to each other in this way?

The Speed of Sound

Does sound take time to travel? Do you hear it the instant it is made? Here is an experiment that will help you to find out.

EXPERIMENT

You will need a drum or a pail.

Go to a large, open place with a friend. Stand near him while he strikes a drum or pail. You seem to hear the sound right away. Now go far away from each other and try again. Do you hear the sound right away, or does it take a little time to reach you? How can you tell? What happens when you go still farther away?

Problem

Thunder is the sound lightning makes. It takes about five seconds for the sound of thunder to travel one mile. With a watch, how can you tell how far away the lightning flashed?

Jet planes fly about six miles high. About how long does it take for the sound of the engines to reach the ground?

Your Ears

What does the doctor see when he looks into your ear? He sees a little sheet of skin called an **eardrum.** Your eardrums are very important parts of your ears. Let's see what they do. Let's build a tin-can eardrum.

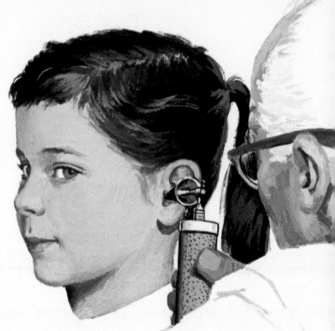

FIND OUT

You will need a tin can with both ends cut out, a rubber balloon, a rubber band, and some dry cereal.

Stretch the balloon across one end of the can. Fasten it with a rubber band. Put three or four pieces of dry cereal on the stretched balloon.

Now ask somebody to say "boom-boom-boom" from underneath. What happens to the cereal? What do sound vibrations do to the stretched balloon?

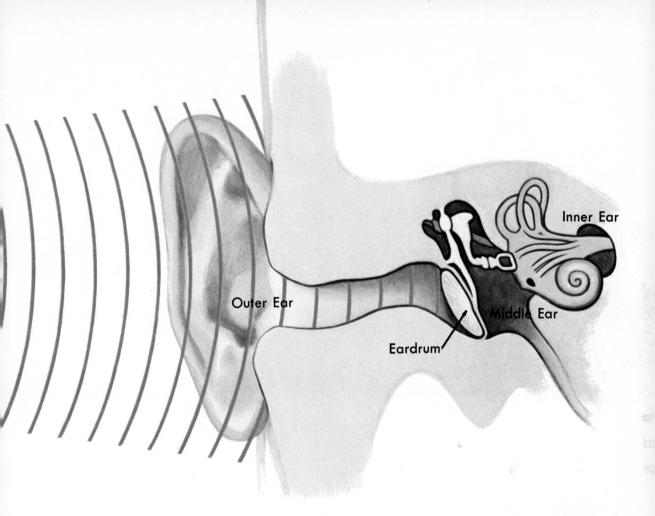

The sheet of rubber is like the eardrum in your ear. Sound vibrations in the air reach your outer ear. The vibrations pass through a tube to the eardrum. This part is called the **middle ear**.

The eardrum conducts the vibrations to three little bones in your middle ear. The bones conduct the vibrations to the inner ear and its nerves that go to your brain. Then you hear.

What would happen if the eardrum were broken?

Sound Comes to Your Ears

Your ears look very nice on you. The rabbit's ears look just as nice on the rabbit. How would it be the other way around? Would you hear differently if you had outer ears as large as a rabbit's? What do you think?

TRY THIS

You will need a sheet of paper and an alarm clock.

Make a paper horn and do this. Stand at one end of the room. At the other end somebody holds a sound-maker such as a ticking alarm clock. Have the person slowly come closer to you. How close is he when you first hear the sound? Measure it.

Now do the same experiment without the paper horn. How close do you hear the sound now?

Stethoscopes

Your doctor listens to sounds inside your body through a stethoscope. How is a stethoscope useful?

A stethoscope has tubes that go to the doctor's ears. You can see how these tubes help.

FIND OUT

You will need a sheet of paper and a watch.

Roll the sheet of paper into a tube. Put the tube over a watch. How well do you hear the ticking of the watch? Now, without changing the distance, listen to the watch without the tube. Can you hear the ticking just as well?

Without the tube, sound vibrations spread out in all directions. Only a small part of each vibration reaches your ears. With the tube the vibrations are conducted to your ear. How does the doctor's stethoscope help him to hear the very soft sounds inside your body?

11

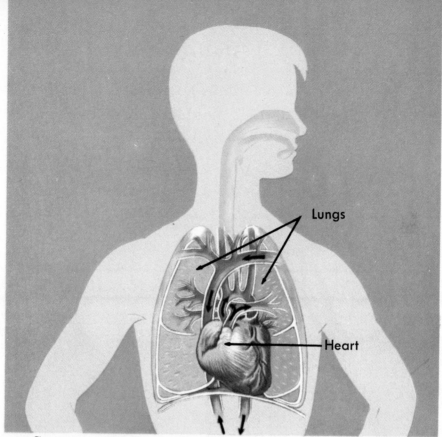

Lungs

Heart

Some parts of your body make very soft sounds as they work.

Your heart makes a lub-dub sound as it pumps blood. You can hear this sound by putting your ear against somebody's chest. The heart is in the middle of the chest near the lungs.

Problem

About how many times a minute does your heart beat? Jump up and down. How does the heartbeat change? How would you find out? Can you hear the sound better with a paper tube?

Your Lungs

Your lungs make a low, windy sound. This is the sound of moving air. Air comes into your nose. It goes through a tube called the **windpipe**. The windpipe branches into your two lungs.

You have muscles that help you breathe. When the muscles press in, they squeeze air *out* of your lungs. You breathe *out,* or exhale.

Then your muscles move back out. Now there is room for fresh air. You breathe *in* fresh air. You inhale. What gas in the air does your body need?

Inhale and exhale.

Feel your chest as you breathe.

In and out, you inhale and exhale. The moving air makes a soft, windy sound.

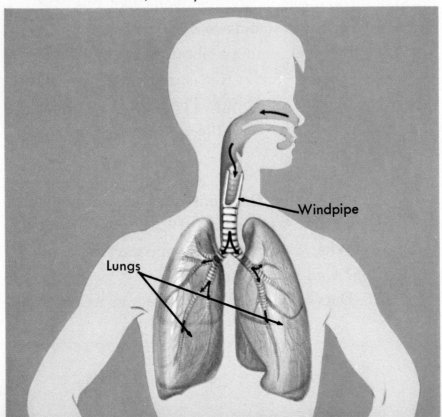

Windpipe

Lungs

String Telephones

You have seen that sound vibrations can travel through a tube. Can they travel through a string?

Make a four-way string telephone like this. Take turns talking and listening to one another.

When you speak, your air vibrations make your cup vibrate. The cup makes the strings vibrate. They make the other cups vibrate. The cups make the air next to them vibrate. Then the other persons hear.

Problem

1. Are sound vibrations conducted through a tight string? A loose string? Can you tell why?

2. What happens when someone touches the string? Can you tell why?

3. Does a longer string conduct as well?

Telephones

Real telephones are joined by wires that carry a steady flow of electricity. This steady flow makes no sound.

1. When you speak into a telephone you make sound vibrations.

2. These vibrations change the steady flow of electricity into vibrations of electricity.

3. You cannot hear these vibrations of electricity, but they zip from one telephone to the other. They travel much faster than the speed of sound—a million times faster!

4. These vibrations of electricity cause a part inside the other telephone to vibrate.

5. This makes the air vibrate. The air vibrates against your eardrum. What happens then?

Study the picture. Find out where each of these five things happens.

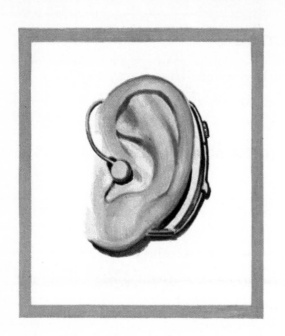

Helping Hearing

Some people do not hear well. This may be because the eardrum does not vibrate well enough.

A hearing aid helps them. It receives sound vibrations and makes them stronger.

Sometimes the trouble is in the conductors. The three little bones in the inner ear may not conduct well enough.

Another kind of hearing aid may be used. This kind receives sound vibrations and makes them stronger, too.

The vibrations are conducted through the bones of the head.

Exploring with Sound

Up in the boat a scientist is listening to the sounds of dolphins. Dolphins are sea mammals. They signal to each other by squeaks, grunts, and whistles.

How does this show, in two ways, that water conducts sound?

Below among the dolphins is a machine that receives sound vibrations. It changes them to electrical vibrations. Where have you used a machine that does this?

The electrical vibrations travel through wires to earphones. How is this like your telephone?

OBSERVE AND FIND OUT

With your teacher, look at the inside of a piano. Find the answers to these questions:

1. When you press a piano key, what makes the piano wire vibrate?
2. In what two ways do the wires look different?
3. In what way do the wires sound different?

FIND OUT FROM OTHERS

1. Go to a building-materials store. Ask about materials that are poor sound conductors. Find out where they are used. Get small pieces of them. Make a chart showing their uses.

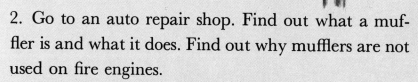

2. Go to an auto repair shop. Find out what a muffler is and what it does. Find out why mufflers are not used on fire engines.
3. Some boats have depth finders to tell how deep the water is. Depth finders work by sound waves. If there is a boat store in your town, find out how a depth finder works. Find out how it can also be used for finding fish.

FIND OUT THROUGH EXPERIMENTS

1. Do sound waves travel better through a pipe or through open air? Get a long piece of garden hose. Whisper into one end while somebody listens at the other end. Can he hear you? Next, whisper without the hose. Can he hear you? Can you explain the difference?

2. Make a one-string guitar like this. You will need a stick, a milk carton, a pencil, a string, and two pushpins or thumbtacks. Tie the string as tight as possible. How do you make loud and soft sounds on it? How do you make deep and high sounds? Can you play a tune on it? Use a thicker string and then a thinner string. How are the sounds different?

3. Push a pin through a paper cup, as in the picture. Put the point of the pin on an old record. Let the record turn. What do you hear? Can you tell how the sound is made?

2
Life in the Desert

A desert in summer is a hot, dry place. In the day-time the ground is very hot. Months go by without a drop of rain. How can anything live in such a place?

Yet many plants and animals do live in the desert. Many different animals make homes, hunt food, and raise their young.

Look at the picture of a desert place in the day-time. Can you see any animal homes? Can you see any animals? What things are alive?

At night it is cool in the desert. The animals that hide in the shade during the hot day come out at night. You have to look sharply to find these animals.

Find the reptiles. Find the mammals. Find the birds. Do you think you will find any fish? How do some of these animals get water? Can you tell some of the ways these animals hide from other animals?

Western Coral Snake

Reptiles in the Desert

There are many reptiles in the desert. A snake is a reptile. Most snakes hatch from eggs.

Here are some desert snakes hatching from eggs! The mother snake laid the eggs in the warm sand. The sand kept the eggs warm until the baby snakes were ready to hatch.

A few kinds of snakes do not lay eggs. The mother keeps the eggs inside of her until the eggs hatch and then the babies are born.

Snakes can take care of themselves as soon as they are born. Do you know some other animals that hatch from eggs? Do they take care of themselves when they hatch?

Has your class ever kept a pet snake? If you touched it, you know that its skin feels hard and dry.

A snake has to crawl over sandy and rocky places. What would happen if a snake's skin were soft like yours? The next experiment will help you answer this question.

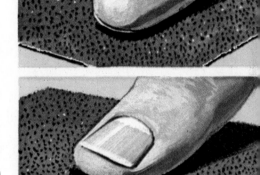

EXPERIMENT

You will need some sand or sandpaper.

Rub your fingernail on some rough sand or sandpaper. Then rub your fingertip across the sand or the sandpaper. Which moved more easily, your fingernail or your fingertip?

A snake's skin is hard like your fingernail. How is a snake's skin good for crawling on sharp sand and rocks? Could a snake with smooth skin and no scales move quickly?

A desert snake's skin helps in other ways. It is made of thick scales which help keep the snake from drying up in the hot sun.

Rattlesnake

23

Here are some other desert reptiles. Tell some ways in which they are alike. Tell some ways in which they are different.

Sidewinder

Chuckwalla

Western Coral Snake

Collared Lizard

Desert Horned Lizard

Desert Tortoise

Gila Monster

Desert Iguana or Crested Lizard

Problem

Find out about some reptiles that:

a) do not live in the desert

b) live in the water

c) live in your part of the country

Mammals of the Desert

This fat little mammal often lives at the edge of the desert. It is called a **prairie dog**. Prairie dogs like to live together in deep tunnels. With their strong feet and sharp claws they dig deep underground.

Like most other mammals, prairie dog babies are born from their mothers. In their underground tunnels, the families are safe from harm.

Like other mammals, the mother prairie dog can feed her babies milk from her own body. Only mammals can make milk for their babies.

Mammals are alike in other ways, too. Their bodies are always warm inside, no matter what kind of weather it is outside. We say mammals are warm-blooded.

25

The bodies of most other animals are warm in warm weather and cold in cold weather. We say these animals are cold-blooded. Fish and frogs, snakes and turtles are all cold-blooded. But prairie dogs and other mammals are warm-blooded.

In its tunnel a prairie dog can hide from anything that likes to eat fat little mammals. And it can hide from something else, too. You can find out what that is by making a tunnel yourself.

EXPERIMENT

You will need a flowerpot full of dry soil, a ruler, and two thermometers.

Poke a hole in the soil about four inches deep. This will be like a little tunnel.

Put one thermometer in the tunnel. Put another thermometer on top of the soil. Put it in just far enough for the earth to cover the bulb of the thermometer. What is the temperature at each place? Write it down.

Put the pot out in the sun. Write down both temperatures every two minutes.

How much difference in temperature is there? Do you think a deeper tunnel would show a still greater difference in temperature? How could you find out?

Problem

Prairie dogs live where it is hot and dry most of the time. Is a deep tunnel a good home for prairie dogs? How?

Here are some other mammals that live in or near the desert in our country.

Find some ways in which they are alike.

Find some ways in which they are different.

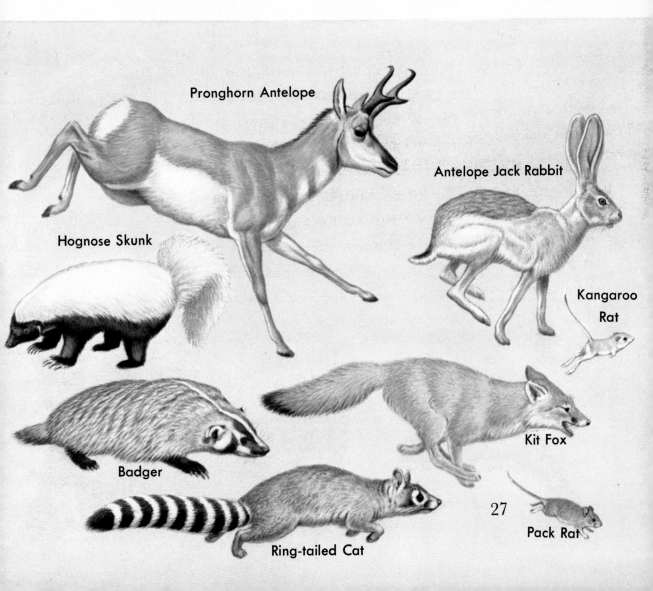

Pronghorn Antelope

Antelope Jack Rabbit

Hognose Skunk

Kangaroo Rat

Badger

Kit Fox

Ring-tailed Cat

Pack Rat

27

Roadrunner

Desert Birds

A roadrunner lives in or near the desert. It is not the most beautiful bird in the world, but it can fight a big snake. It can kill it and eat it. A roadrunner catches lizards, too. With its long, sharp bill it reaches into cracks between rocks.

Its long, pointed claws are good for running over sand.

Find out about these other desert birds.

What homes do they have?

What do they feed their babies?

Verdin

Desert Sparrow

Elf Owl

Vermilion Flycatcher

28

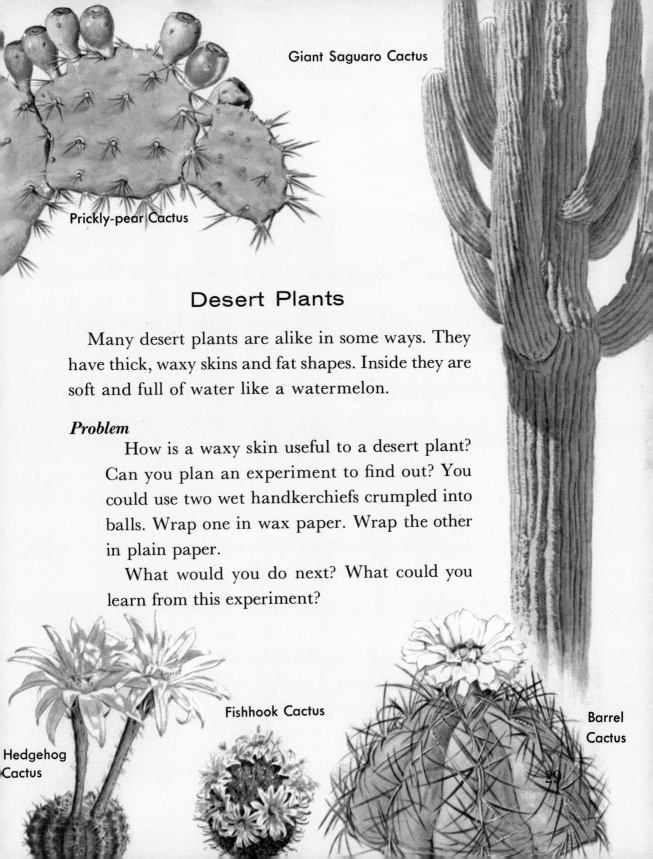

Giant Saguaro Cactus

Prickly-pear Cactus

Desert Plants

Many desert plants are alike in some ways. They have thick, waxy skins and fat shapes. Inside they are soft and full of water like a watermelon.

Problem

How is a waxy skin useful to a desert plant? Can you plan an experiment to find out? You could use two wet handkerchiefs crumpled into balls. Wrap one in wax paper. Wrap the other in plain paper.

What would you do next? What could you learn from this experiment?

Hedgehog Cactus

Fishhook Cactus

Barrel Cactus

29

How is a fat shape useful to a desert plant?
Here is a way to find out.

EXPERIMENT

You will need a clothes hanger, two handkerchiefs, and water.

The clothes hanger will be your scale. Get two handkerchiefs of the same size. Wet both. Crumple one into a round ball. Leave the other handkerchief flat and straight. Hang both handkerchiefs up, as in the picture.

Which is like the fat shape of the cactus? What do you think will probably happen to the water in each handkerchief? Give your reasons.

Now observe the results of your experiment. Which handkerchief became lighter? How can you tell? From which handkerchief did the water evaporate faster? Which shape is better for keeping water?

Desert soil has very little water. But desert plants have long roots that spread all around. This helps them get what little water there is in the soil.

Now can you tell how each of these is useful to a desert plant: A fat, round shape? A waxy skin? Long, slender roots?

30

Many desert plants have sharp spines. The spines keep many animals from eating the plants. But some little animals do eat them. The little animals can run up and down and in between the sharp spines without getting hurt. Some animals even make their homes in the cactus.

Here are some plants and animals that live in the desert.

How do some of them keep cool?

How do some find food? Homes? Water?

Not everything can live in the desert. Plants and animals must have special ways of living in hot, dry, desert places. But people can live almost anywhere on earth.

31

DISCUSS AND FIND OUT

1. What would you need for a one-week camping trip in the desert? Think about the hot days, the cold nights, and the supply of water. Discuss your food, clothing, water supply, and shelter.

2. Pretend you are one of the desert animals. Tell about how you live comfortably in the desert.

3. Look carefully at a cactus plant. Then look at a geranium or some other plant that grows in your home or classroom. Talk about the differences you see between the desert plant and the one that does not grow in the desert.

FIND OUT THROUGH EXPERIMENTS

1. Make two desert gardens like these. What kind of soil will you use? What kind of plants? Keep one moist all the time and the other one quite dry. Keep a chart of how they grow.

2. Cut out two paper rabbits like the picture. Make them almost as big as this page. Cut one from white paper and one from brown paper. Place one cutout rabbit on white paper and the other on brown paper. Then change them around. Look at them again. Do they look different? Why?

FIND OUT FROM BOOKS

1. Find out about the color changes of some animals. Does change in color help these animals? If so, how?

2. Read about some trees that live in the desert. Are they different from trees that live in your neighborhood? How?

3. Find out about some Indians who live in the desert. How do they get their food? How do they get their water? Where do they live?

4. In what deserts does this animal live? Why is it such a useful animal?

34

3
A Pond Community

Have you ever visited a place like this? It is very quiet! It seems as if you are alone. But there are many animals that live here.

Different plants and animals can live in different kinds of places on the earth's surface. Many plants and animals live near ponds and streams. Under the water, too, is a busy world of living things.

35

The plants and animals that live together in and near a pond are part of a community. There are many different living things in this pond community.

Look at the picture.

Find a mammal.

What does it eat?

Find some fish.

Find some birds. Can you find a nest?

Find a frog. A frog is an amphibian.

Find some insects.

Swallows

Cattails

Bittern

Tadpoles

Snapping Turtle

Muskrat

36

Find some animals that eat plants.

Which animals eat insects?

Which animals eat animals larger than insects?

Can you see animals hiding among the plants?

Find some animals that make their homes among the plants.

Every animal and plant gives something to its community. Every animal and plant gets something from its community.

As you study this chapter, try to see what each living thing gives to its community. Find out what it gets from its community.

Dragonfly

Grebe

Water Lilies

Bullfrog

Otter

Sunfish

Catfish

Color That Protects

Find a frog in the picture on page 37. Was it easy to find the frog?

A green frog on a green plant can sit and catch insects with its long tongue. A bird flying overhead, looking for a frog to eat, cannot easily see the frog.

But look at the underside of the frog. It is almost white.

Does its color protect the frog? You can find out.

TRY THIS

You will need two sheets of paper, one dark and one light.

Take the light and dark sheets of paper outside and hold them over your head. Which one is harder to see against the bright sky?

Fishes and birds both eat frogs. How does the light color of its underside protect a frog from animals under it? How does its green color protect a frog from animals above it?

Colors that protect an animal are called **protective coloration**. Which animals on pages 34–37 have protective coloration? Can you explain why some animals' color is not a protection?

Here are some other animals that live in or near
the pond. These animals have protective coloration.
Discuss how each animal's color is a protection.

Female Red-winged Blackbird — with young

Marsh Rabbit

Dragonfly

Mud Turtle

Green Sunfish

Brown Trout

39

Blue Heron

Coot

Osprey

Bird Feet

Birds use their feet in different ways. All birds can walk, but some can also swim. Some birds catch food with their feet. Look at the birds below. How do their feet work like the things next to them?

40

Coot

Pelican

Red-winged Blackbird

Pintail

Bird Bills

Many kinds of birds live at the pond. They eat different kinds of food. They have different kinds of bills for getting food. Here are some pond birds. How does each bill work like the tool shown next to it?

Water Birds

Water birds have oily feathers, and they have ways of keeping their feathers oiled. You can find out how oil helps a water bird.

EXPERIMENT

You will need newspaper, oil, a ruler, string, and water.

Cut two small pieces of newspaper. Rub oil on one piece. Attach them to a ruler to make a scale. Balance them by snipping pieces from the heavy side.

Dip both sides into water. Lift them out of the water. Which side is heavier? Why? What would happen to a water bird's feathers if they were not oily?

Water birds have different ways that help them live on or near water. What are some of these ways? List the ways these birds are like all other birds.

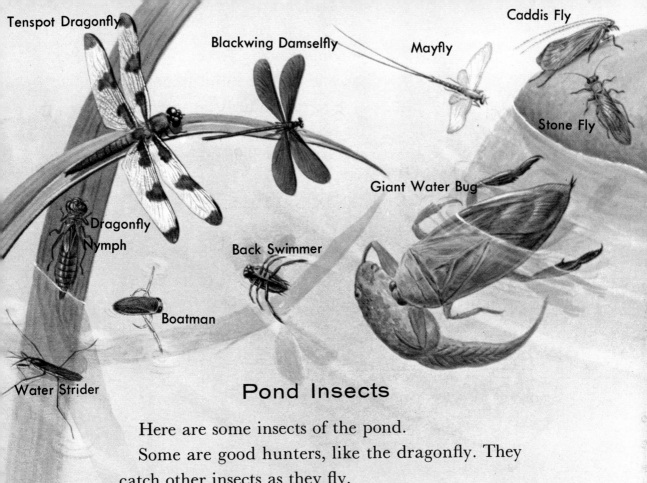

Tenspot Dragonfly

Blackwing Damselfly

Mayfly

Caddis Fly

Stone Fly

Dragonfly Nymph

Back Swimmer

Giant Water Bug

Boatman

Water Strider

Pond Insects

Here are some insects of the pond.

Some are good hunters, like the dragonfly. They catch other insects as they fly.

Some are strong swimmers, like the water skater. They catch other insects as they swim.

Some insects live in the muddy bottom of the pond. The big water bug swims along the muddy bottom and catches small fish and frogs.

Wherever you see many insects, you can be sure there is plenty of food for birds and fish and frogs.

You can be sure there is plenty of food for insects, too. Insects that eat other insects can find plenty of food in the pond. Insects that eat plants can find them in the pond.

Caddis Fly Larvae

Mayfly Nymph

Stone Fly Nymph

43

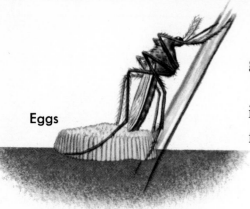

Eggs

Some insects lay eggs on plants that grow in the water and around the pond.

The mosquito is an insect that lays its eggs right on the water. The eggs float on the water.

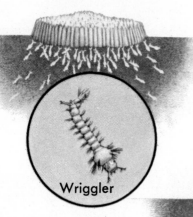

Wriggler

After a while, tiny wrigglers hatch out of the eggs.

The wriggler swims in the pond to get food. After a few days of feeding, it changes its shape. It becomes a **pupa.**

Pupa

After two days the pupa becomes a full-grown mosquito and bites its way out of the cover.

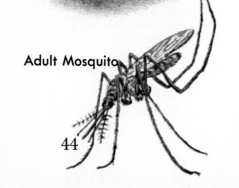

Adult Mosquito

Tell some ways you know that the mosquito is harmful.

44

All the animals and plants in the pond depend on one another for food. There is something else that all living things need that you cannot see. No matter where they live, plants and animals need air.

There are two parts of the air that are important to living things. Let's find out about them.

Oxygen and Carbon Dioxide

Oxygen is a gas. It is the part of the air that animals need in order to live. Fish live in water, but they must have air from which they can get oxygen.

Is there air in water? Here is how you can find out.

TRY THIS

You will need a glass of water.

Fill the drinking glass with water.

Let it stand for a while.

Then look at it. What do you see along the inside of the glass?

These are bubbles of air that came out of the water. You cannot use oxygen from air that is in water, but a fish can.

45

A fish gets oxygen through special parts called **gills**. Water with air in it passes over the gills. Gills take oxygen from the air in the water. So fish do not have to come up for air.

At the same time as the fish takes in oxygen, something else happens. **Carbon dioxide** goes out of the gills into the water. Carbon dioxide is a gas. It is a very important part of the air.

The same thing happens with other water animals. They take in oxygen from the air in water. They give back carbon dioxide to the water.

The same thing happens on land, too. Birds, bugs, all living things take oxygen from the air. They all give back carbon dioxide to the air.

You can show that you give off carbon dioxide. There is a way to test for this gas. On page 268 you can find out about the carbon dioxide test.

Yellow Perch

But why is carbon dioxide important? Green plants use it! They put carbon dioxide together with water and make food out of it. This happens when sunlight shines on the plants. They make food, and at the same time they give off oxygen. Who uses the oxygen?

Look at the little community in the picture. Can you answer these questions about it?

What gas do the plants take in to make food?

Where does this gas come from?

When plants make food, what gas do they give off?

What gas do animals need? Where do they get it?

Answer these questions for living things on land.

Think about communities again. Everything gives something; everything takes something. Can we say that all the living things of the world are part of a community?

Beaver lodge

Beaver

Mammals in the Pond Community

Here is a beaver being as busy as a beaver. It is busy cutting down a tree with its sharp teeth. It is making a safe, dry home out in the water. Animals that hunt beavers cannot easily get into the beaver's home because the opening is under water. When the pond is frozen over, the beaver is very safe.

Moose

Mink

Muskrat

Raccoon

Otter

Rat

With its webfeet and wide tail, the beaver is a good swimmer. It also uses its tail for something else. When it slaps its tail on the water, the little beavers hear the sound and hurry home.

Find the other mammals of the pond community.

In what ways are these mammals alike?

In what ways are mammals part of the community?

Soilmakers

On a windy night, a few years ago, something joined the pond community. With a loud crash, a dead tree came smashing down.

This was not the first time that such a thing had happened. The pond and the forest have been here a long time. Thousands of trees have lived and grown and died here.

Where are they all? Why isn't the forest heaped high with dead trees?

Skunk Cabbage

Black-and-white Warbler

Ghost Pipes

50

Fiddleheads
(new fern leaves)

Skunk

Insect Grubs

Bracken Fungi

Look at a dead tree on the forest floor. There are millions of plants and animals busily at work on it. When they are through, the dead tree will be part of the soil.

Let's see how this can happen.

51

Fungi

Carpenter Ants

Insects and Soil

Some black ants are making their home in the dead tree. The ants chew out little tunnels to live in. They lay eggs and raise their young in the tunnels. Look at the little heap of sawdust underneath the tree. Can you guess how it was made?

Wind and rain will mix the sawdust into the soil. A little bit of the tree will become part of the soil.

Two birds are hunting for beetle grubs under the bark. The birds peck holes with their bills. Then they pull out the grubs and eat them.

The holes let water and air inside. The wood begins to soften and crumble and break apart. Then gravity takes the pieces away. What do you think will happen next?

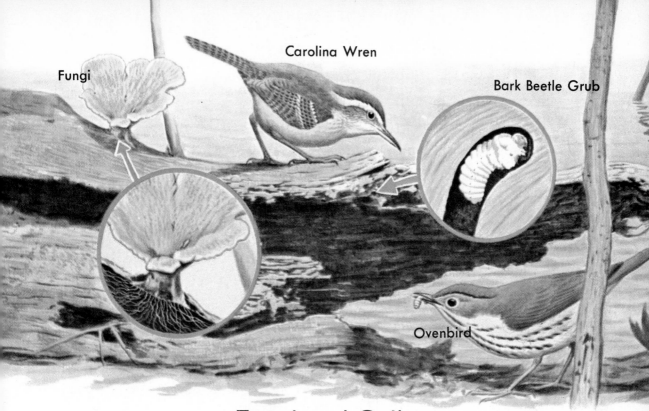

Fungi

Carolina Wren

Bark Beetle Grub

Ovenbird

Fungi and Soil

Here are some fungi that feed on the dead tree.
Fungi are living plants, but they cannot make food.
They live on food in other plants and animals.

You may have seen some fungi like these.

You can grow a fungus and observe it. The fungus
that you can grow is called bread mold.

EXPERIMENT

You will need a loaf of bread, wax paper, a dish with a cover, a magnifying lens, and water.

Unwrap a loaf of bread. Quickly wrap one slice in wax paper. Dampen another slice. Let it stay in the open dish for an hour. Then cover the dish and leave it in a warm, dark place for a few days.

Look at both slices. Do you find fuzzy growths like this? On which slice do you find them?

Under a magnifying lens they look like this. The round, dark knobs are full of tiny dots called **spores.**

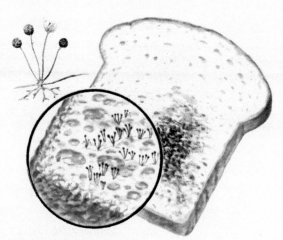

Spores are something like seeds. When they are ripe, they fall out. They are very tiny and light. Moving air carries them around like dust. If they fall in the right places, they grow. All fungi, even large mushrooms, grow from tiny spores.

Problem

How did bread mold get started on your slice of bread?

How did the fungi on the dead tree get their start? Are the mushrooms on page 55 helpful in making soil? Are some of them harmful to you?

Common Shelf Fungus

Common Morel

Common Meadow Mushroom

Parasol Mushroom

Brownie Caps

Cup-shaped Puffball

Fly Amanita

Coral Fungus

Death-cup Amanita

Jack-o'-lantern

Boletus

55

Other living things also help break down dead plants. These are bacteria. Like fungi, bacteria do not make their own food. They live and feed on plant and animal materials. When something rots, it is being broken apart by bacteria and fungi.

In the woods is rotting useful or harmful?

In a fruit store is rotting useful or harmful?

Growing Plants and Soil

Green plants take root in the dead tree. First there were spores or seeds that fell on the tree. Little roots began to push into the wood. The roots made little tunnels and crumbled the wood into bits.

Find a plant like one of these. Pull away a tiny bit. What do you find among the roots? How do plant roots help make soil?

Each living thing gets something from the community. Each living thing gives something back to the community.

56

Making a Water Community

Have you ever wished you could see what goes on down below the surface of a pond? You can have your wish if you make a pond of your own in a glass tank. Such an indoor pond is called an **aquarium**.

You can buy the things you need to fill your aquarium from a pet shop. Or, if you can get some help, you may be able to get them in a pond or lake.

TRY THIS

You will need a very clean glass tank, washed sand, water plants, water animals, and water. A water pump is also useful if you have one.

Put in about two inches of sand. Put a sheet of paper on it. Pour water over the paper. Pour in enough water to cover the sand by two or three inches.

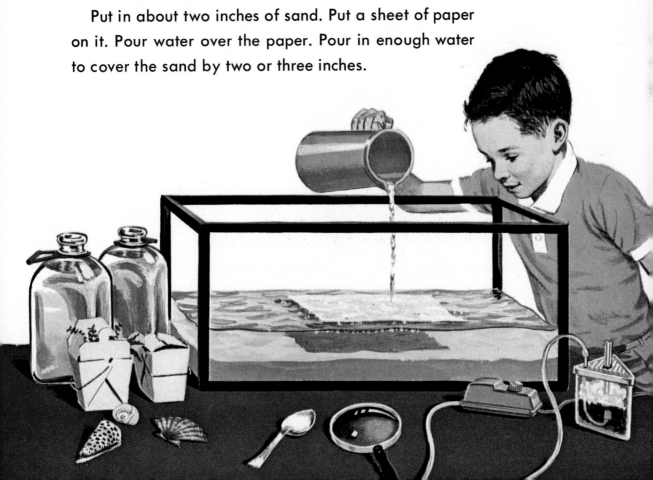

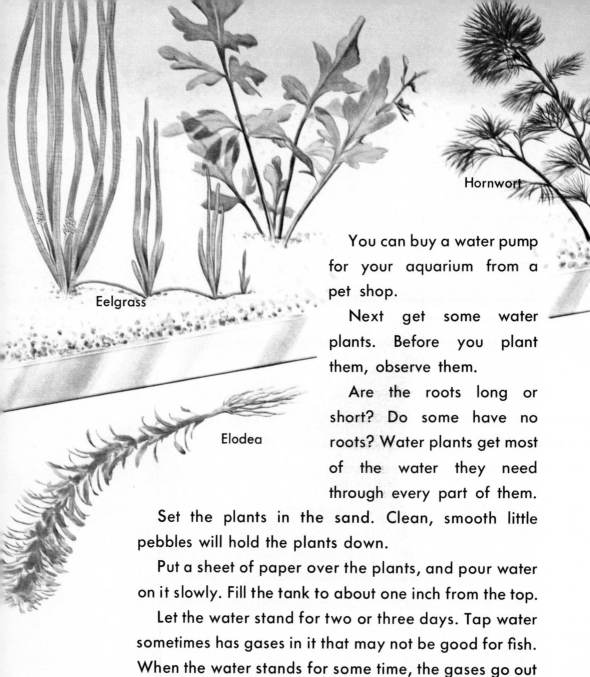

Eelgrass

Elodea

Hornwort

You can buy a water pump for your aquarium from a pet shop.

Next get some water plants. Before you plant them, observe them.

Are the roots long or short? Do some have no roots? Water plants get most of the water they need through every part of them.

Set the plants in the sand. Clean, smooth little pebbles will hold the plants down.

Put a sheet of paper over the plants, and pour water on it slowly. Fill the tank to about one inch from the top.

Let the water stand for two or three days. Tap water sometimes has gases in it that may not be good for fish. When the water stands for some time, the gases go out into the air.

Water plants need a few hours of light each day. They can use light from the sun or from a tank light.

58

Snails in the Aquarium

Now you are ready for your first water animals. Get some black snails. Put them in the aquarium.

Observe the snails crawling along. They have feelers that help them find out about the things ahead of them. Gently touch the tip of a feeler with a pencil. How does the snail protect itself?

Snails' eyes can tell light from dark, but cannot see things. You can get an idea of what this is like by looking through wax paper.

Tap a snail when it is floating. Watch how it sinks. It lets out a bubble of air and takes in a drop of water. This makes the snail heavier than water and it sinks.

How does the snail crawl along? What does the snail do as it moves up and down and around the tank? The snails are useful in this community. They help keep the water clear. They eat the tiny green plants that grow on the sides and bottom of the tank.

Do you think snails are useful in a pond or lake?

59

Egg capsules on leaf

Egg capsule with young

Young Snails

Ramshorn Snail

The Life Cycle of a Snail

The snails in your aquarium may lay eggs. You may see little patches on the glass that look like tiny bits of jelly. These are snail eggs. Watch them for a few days. Do you see tiny spots on them? With a magnifying lens you can see that these tiny spots are baby snails inside the eggs.

The eggs will hatch. The baby snails will grow. They will lay eggs. What will happen then?

Pond Snail

Fish in the Aquarium

When your aquarium is ready, buy the fish. Guppies are good fish to buy. You must feed them because your aquarium does not have the food that guppies find in ponds or streams. Find out at the pet shop how to keep the water at the right temperature.

Your guppies may have babies. First, the mother guppy's body will get bigger. You will see a black spot where the babies are growing.

Most fish lay eggs in the water. Then the eggs hatch. But guppies keep the eggs in their bodies. They hatch inside. Then the baby fish are born.

Look at the shape of a fish. See how the fish pushes itself by waving its tail. How does it use its fins for stopping? See the smooth, shiny scales. How are they useful?

Watch the fish move its mouth. Each mouthful of water flows over the gills and out through the opened gill covers. What gas does the fish get from the water? What gas does the fish put into the water? How does this help the plants?

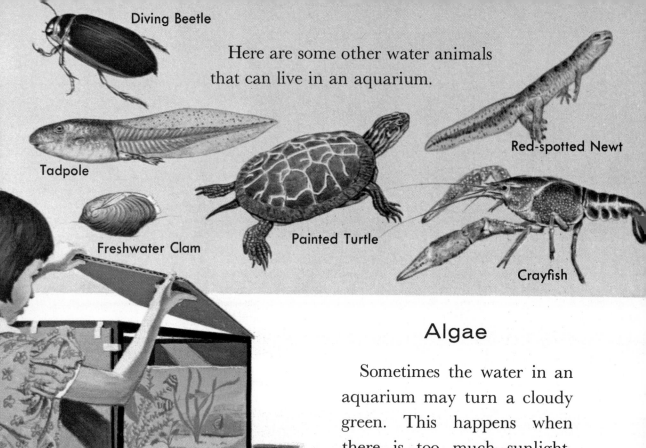

Diving Beetle

Here are some other water animals that can live in an aquarium.

Red-spotted Newt

Tadpole

Freshwater Clam

Painted Turtle

Crayfish

Algae

Sometimes the water in an aquarium may turn a cloudy green. This happens when there is too much sunlight. Fasten a piece of cardboard to the side of the glass. It will keep out some sunlight.

The green color comes from tiny plants called **algae.** Some algae were on the aquarium plants when you got them. Like all green plants, algae take in carbon dioxide. They make food with it. They grow. They give off oxygen.

The algae are not harmful. Snails eat some, and so do some fish. But there can be too much of one kind of thing in a community. So we cut down on the sunlight. This cuts down on the algae.

62

An aquarium is a little community. Each living thing in it gets something. Each living thing gives something.

What do animals in the community get from plants? What do they give to the plants? What do plants get? What do they give?

Over and over again, carbon dioxide goes from animals to plants. Over and over again, food and oxygen go from plants to animals. With sunlight to keep the plants growing, the cycle keeps going around and around.

Your aquarium is a little world. Does the same cycle happen in your big world?

DISCUSS AND FIND OUT

1. Make a chart or a class bulletin board like the one below:

	Around the pond	On the pond	In the water
Plants			
Animals			

   Name and talk about some plants and animals that live in each part of the community. What happens in each part during the winter?

2. Find out what insects in the pond are harmful to people. How are they kept from harming us?

3. What do plants and animals give to the pond community? What do they get from it?

DO THIS AND FIND OUT

1. Make a book of bird pictures. Show how the bills and feet of birds help them get the food they need.

2. Gather plants from a pond. Arrange them in a container of pond water. Which ones live on top of the water? Which ones have only their roots in the water? Which ones live all the way under the water?

3. Set up an aquarium. Have fish, snails, and (maybe) tadpoles. How does each one move? Does a fish have ears? Can a fish close its eyes? How does it sleep? What does a snail eat? If you have tadpoles, what happens to them?

FIND OUT FROM BOOKS

What are some ways in which each of these animals protects itself? Where does it live? What does it eat?

4
The Big Ocean

Have you ever been to the seashore? Have you looked out over the ocean and wondered how big it is?

Have you ever tasted water from the ocean? When you get a mouthful of salty ocean water, you may wonder, "How does it get so salty anyway?"

There are so many things to make you wonder—the waves, the sand, the strange shells and seaweed, the long-legged little birds that run right into the curl of the waves. Let's wonder about the ocean.

67

Does the ocean have an end? We could find out by sailing a boat around the world. But we might not get home in time for dinner, so let's sail a paper boat around a globe.

TRY THIS

Make a paper boat. Put it on the globe near land. Sail it away from the land. Look for the end of the ocean. Look for a place where you cannot sail around the land to another part of the ocean. Can you find such a place?

All the oceans of the world are really one big ocean.

These children are coloring the parts of the world
that are covered by the oceans. Somewhere in each
ocean there is a place where the water is joined to
the water of another ocean. The big ocean has no
end. This big ocean covers three times as much of
the earth's surface as all the land.

Look at these maps. They are really flattened-out
pictures of the globe on which you sailed your little
boat. Can you find the parts of the globe on these
maps? Can you find our country? Can you find the
places where you sailed your little boat?

Why Is the Ocean Salty?

Scientists do not know all the reasons why the ocean is salty. But they do know that some of the salt came from the land.

How did this happen? You know that most rivers flow into the ocean. As each river empties into the ocean, it carries a little salt with it. Where did this salt come from?

There is a little salt in some rocks and soils. Salt is a mineral. A mineral is a material of the earth that is neither plant nor animal. Rocks are made up of one or more kinds of minerals. Some minerals dissolve in water. Do you think salt dissolves in water? Try it.

When rain falls on rocks and soil, it dissolves tiny bits of some minerals and carries them away. This experiment gives an idea of how this happens.

EXPERIMENT

You will need sand, a glass jar, two milk cartons, a large needle, salt, two small paper cups, blocks of wood, water, and a measuring cup.

Wash some sand by putting it into a glass jar with clean water. Stir the sand. Let it stand. Pour off the water. Do this several times.

Cut off the tops of two milk cartons. With a large needle, put a few holes in the bottom of each. Put a cupful of clean, washed sand in each. Mix a teaspoonful of salt with the sand in one of the cartons.

Put both cartons on blocks of wood like this. Pour a half cup of water into each carton. Let the water trickle through. Then take a tiny taste of the water in each cup. Is the taste the same?

Why did you use two cartons of sand? Can you see the salt in the water?

Something like this happens when rain falls on the
soil. Of course, the soil is not so full of salt as the sand
in your experiment was. There is only a very, very
little here and there.

As rain falls, some of the water seeps through the
ground. It dissolves some minerals, just as it did in
your experiment.

Some of the water flows underground and some of
it flows above ground. The underground and ground
waters, with their load of dissolved minerals, flow
until they join rivers. The rivers flow on and on until
at last they flow into the ocean.

Rivers carry the salt and other minerals into the
ocean. The salt gives ocean water its salty taste.

River water usually has some salt dissolved in it, but river water does not taste salty. River water flows into the ocean, yet ocean water does taste salty.

Why is the ocean saltier than the rivers that flow into it? Let's find out how this can be.

EXPERIMENT

You will need two bowls of the same size, a cover for one of them, a measuring cup, water, and salt.

Pour a cup of water into each bowl. Dissolve one-half teaspoonful of salt in each of the bowls. Taste the water in each bowl. Does it taste the same?

Cover one bowl. Set both bowls in a warm, sunny place. Draw a line at the water level on each bowl.

Let both bowls stand for two days or more. Then dip up a spoonful of water from each. Taste each spoonful.

Which water tastes saltier? Which bowl has less water? What happened to the water in the open bowl? Did any of the water in the covered bowl evaporate?

Something like this happens in the ocean. The sun shining on the ocean makes the water evaporate. The salt does not evaporate. It stays in the ocean.

Day after day, year after year, the rivers of the world pour into the ocean. The river water has tiny amounts of salt in it, but not enough to taste. As it flows into the ocean, the water keeps evaporating, but the salt remains. That is why the ocean is saltier than the rivers that flow into it.

Suppose salty river water kept coming into a lake. Suppose the water kept evaporating. What would happen to the saltiness of the lake water?

There are some very salty lakes. One is the Great Salt Lake in Utah.

Minerals from the Ocean

Look back to the experiment on page 73. What will happen if you let the water keep on evaporating? Try it and see.

EXPERIMENT

You will need some water, salt, and a bowl or pan.

Pour salt water into an open pan or bowl and let it stand in the sun. (If you are in a hurry, you may boil the water.)

What happens to the water? What is left behind?

Does this give you an idea? Could this be a way to get salt from the ocean?

It could indeed, and people do it in many parts of the world. They let ocean water flow over flat beaches. They build low walls of sand or soil to keep the water from flowing back into the ocean.

The water is evaporated by the heat of the sun. Dry salt and other minerals are left behind on the beach.

There are salt mines in some underground places. These places were once shallow seas. The water evaporated, but the salt remained behind. Later, the soil became covered with rock, sand, and soil.

The salt in your salt shaker probably came from an underground salt mine. But salt has many other uses besides its use in food. Find out about some of these uses. Salt is a very important mineral.

Scientists have discovered many kinds of minerals in the oceans of the world. There are huge amounts of iron, copper, nickel, and other useful minerals. Some of these are found as lumps on the ocean floor.

Scientists think that these minerals can be mined. They are planning to scoop them up with machines that look like huge vacuum cleaners. The minerals would be pumped up and loaded into ships.

77

The ocean is part of the earth's cover. The land beneath the ocean has mountains, valleys, and plains. Scientists know some things about the plants, minerals, and animals in the sea. But a great deal is not known.

Oceanographers are scientists who study the ocean. They are finding out more about the ocean bottom with many new kinds of instruments.

Oceanographers are trying to find more food and more minerals for the world.

78

Plants and Animals of the Sea

The sea is full of food and minerals. You know that plants are food for many kinds of animals. Scientists know that plants from the sea are food for the millions of animals of the sea. They think that these plants could be used as food for people, too.

But when you stand at the seashore and look out at the sea, you see hardly any plants. You may see a bit of seaweed drift by. In shallow places near the shore there may be some sea plants growing. That seems to be about all.

Yet the sea is full of plants. Some that grow near the shore are quite large. But most of the plants that grow in the sea are so small that you cannot see them.

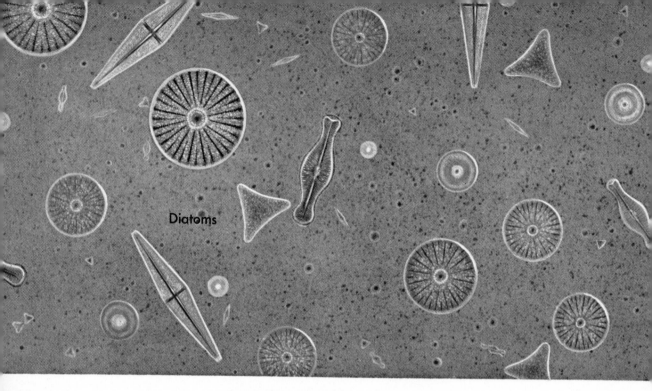

Diatoms

Tiny Plants in the Sea

There are millions of plants in a glass of seawater. They are tiny green plants called algae. The picture shows the algae much larger than they are. You cannot see algae, but all the animals of the sea depend on them. The algae float in the water. They take in minerals from the water. They also take in carbon dioxide that is dissolved in the water. The sun shines on the green algae. They make food and grow.

Tiny water animals eat the tiny algae. Bigger animals eat the animals that eat algae. And these bigger animals are food of still other animals. So you see that no matter what food a sea animal eats, it depends on the food made by green plants.

If you visit a fish market, you can see a few of the many, many different kinds of animals that come from the sea.

There are fish in many colors and shapes and sizes. There are shelled animals, such as oysters, which look like ragged rocks, and scallops shaped like pretty little fans. Perhaps you have been a little frightened by a lobster waving a huge claw, or a crab that suddenly clicked its blue legs.

In some markets you can see even stranger sea animals. Squids and octopuses, shrimps and snails, clams and mussels—all these are only a few of the sea animals that are sold as food.

81

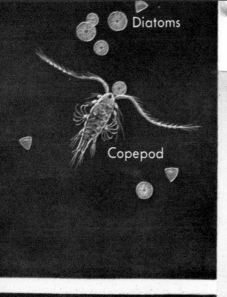

Diatoms

Copepod

Copepod

Young Herring

Herring

Squid

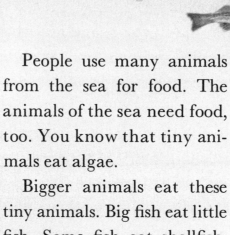

Herring

Cod

People use many animals from the sea for food. The animals of the sea need food, too. You know that tiny animals eat algae.

Bigger animals eat these tiny animals. Big fish eat little fish. Some fish eat shellfish. Some animals eat the young of other animals. People eat both plants and animals from the ocean.

Find some animals that are eating plants. Find some animals that are eating other animals.

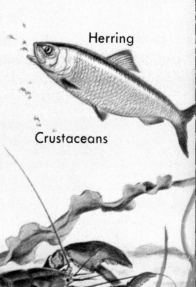

Herring

Crustaceans

Lobster

Starfish

Oyster

82

The Life Cycle of Salmon

To catch large numbers of sea animals, a fisherman must know their ways. He must know where they go, to find them when they are big enough to be used for food. He must know how they grow, from the time they are born to the time they have young. This is called the life cycle.

One of the important food fish is salmon. Fishermen have learned about the life cycle of the salmon.

Salmon live in the ocean, far from land. They come to rivers only when they are ready to lay eggs. Fishermen know what time of year the salmon come. They catch some of the big ones for food.

In the quiet water of brooks and pools, salmon lay their eggs.

Salmon laying eggs

When the baby salmon hatch out of the eggs, they live in the brooks and fresh-water streams, eating and growing.

Minnows

Then the young salmon swim out into the ocean.

Young Fry

Sockeye

When the salmon are fully grown, they swim back to the very same streams where they were born. They lay their eggs. What happens next?

This is the life cycle of salmon. Like most fish, they lay eggs, the young hatch, they grow, they lay eggs. Over and over, this happens. Over and over they go through their life cycle.

84

Mammals of the Sea

The biggest animal on land or sea is the whale. It seems to be a large fish, but it is a mammal. A fish can get oxygen from water. But a mammal must take in oxygen from the air.

TRY THIS

You are a mammal. How many breaths do you take in a minute? Is there a difference when you are still? When you jump? How long can you hold your breath?

You might be able to inhale enough air to stay under water about half a minute. Then you must come up and exhale.

Whales can stay under water for fifteen minutes. But then they must come up and exhale. What a huge breath!

The huge breath of a whale makes a big spout. It looks like a cloud. Can you tell why? Think of your breath on a cold morning.

Whales are different from fish in other ways. Can you tell what the ways are?

In the old days whaling was dangerous work. But whales were valuable. They had thick layers of fat called blubber. The blubber was boiled into whale oil. The oil was used in lamps.

Today whaling is much safer. Fleets of fast ships hunt the whales. The whales are towed to large factory ships. Most of the work is done by machines.

Almost every part of the whale is used. The oil from blubber is made into margarine, machine oil, and soap. The meat is good to eat. The liver contains vitamins. Some parts are made into fertilizer and some parts are made into perfume!

Whales are not the only mammals in the ocean. Some others are shown on the next page.

Mammals of the Sea

Seals

Walrus

Dolphin

Sea Otter

Sea Cow

Killer Whale

Life in the Sea

The sea is full of life. Animals of many kinds float and drift and swim about in it. There are fish, mammals, reptiles, and birds. There are animals you may never have seen: squids, sea cucumbers, razor clams, jellyfish, sponges, moon snails, and swimming worms. There are tiny animals, like those circled above.

There is plenty of plant life in the sea. Red and green seaweeds cling to the rocks in shallow waters. Long brown ribbons of kelp drift on the waves. And there are billions of tiny algae like those in the circle on page 89. All these sea plants live near the surface, where the sunlight reaches them.

Most of the life of the sea is near the surface. Can you tell why?

Sunlight can reach only a few hundred feet down in seawater. Below that it is pitch dark all the way down. Some places are more than six miles deep! Plants cannot grow in this endless night.

And yet some kinds of sea animals live there. Some feed on dead animals that sink down from the surface. Others feed on living animals of the deep. There are fish lit up with tiny glowing dots. There are fish with lights like little lanterns.

Oceanographers have discovered undersea mountains thousands of feet high. They have mapped deep valleys miles below the surface. With special undersea cameras they take pictures of animals that nobody has ever seen before.

What other strange and wonderful things will they discover? All of us wait for the news.

89

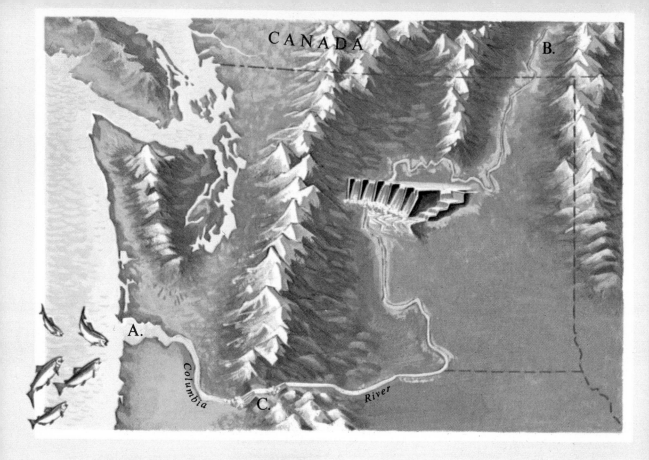

DISCUSS AND FIND OUT

1. Why is the line marking the Columbia River thicker at A than at B? Does the river flow from A to B or from B to A?

2. Is the water saltier at A or at B? Why?

3. There are mountains in the area. How can the river flow between mountain ranges?

4. Salmon come in from the sea into the river. Does the flow of the water help the fish? Or do they have to fight against it?

5. There is a waterfall at C. Do the salmon jump up it or do they fall over it before they swim on?

FIND OUT THROUGH EXPERIMENTS

1. Salt is sometimes put on icy sidewalks. Find out what salt does to ice. You will need two ice cubes. Which cube of ice melts sooner?

2. Place one ice cube in a glass of water. Does it float on top of the water? Or is most of it under the water? Where are there large pieces of ice floating in the ocean? What are they called? Are they dangerous? If so, why?

3. Put a small container of fresh water and a small container of salty water in the freezer. Which one freezes first? Why?

FIND OUT FROM BOOKS

1. Find out about other animals that live in the ocean. What are some ways in which they are different from land animals?

2. What other mammals besides whales live in the sea? What are some ways in which sea mammals are different from fish?

3. What are some ways in which the sea is important to us? Is it getting to be more important to us each year? How?

5
Plants and More Plants

Look at the seeds in a single plant! One pumpkin, one tomato, one maple tree, one corn ear, one stalk of wheat—almost any plant you can think of makes lots and lots of seeds.

Look at one of these plants. Think of it! Each of those seeds could become a plant. It doesn't happen, of course, but why not? Make a few guesses.

Now let's look at one dandelion to see what happens to its seeds. Here it is, with a hundred seeds ready to go as soon as the wind blows them.

On your mark, get set, blow!

93

This little dandelion seed went to market—a supermarket. It landed on a can of beans. No soil, no water, no place to grow, so the dandelion didn't grow.

This seed landed on a little lake. There was plenty of water, but no soil. Nothing happened.

This seed landed in a pinch of damp soil in a crack in the sidewalk. Soil and water! It began to grow, and then somebody stepped on it. That finished it.

And the same sort of thing happened to most of the other dandelion seeds. You could make up a few stories yourself.

Maybe two or three seeds landed in a good place. They grew into dandelion plants and made hundreds of seeds. But now you know why hundreds of seeds don't always become hundreds of plants.

Bring in some plants with seeds. How many seeds are there? Tell in what ways some of them could have become plants. Use these carriers in your answers: wind, water, animals, man.

94

New Plants from Old Plants

New plants can also be made without seeds. You can usually see this in an empty lot.

Find a place where the soil was dug away some time ago. Have some plants begun to grow? Perhaps they look like these. You can see that there are new plants growing in the bare soil.

How did all the new plants get there?

What parts of the plant will help you find out?

You will need a small clump of grass.

Rinse the roots to wash off the soil. Do you find separate little plants, or are some of them joined like this?

A grass plant sends out roots. One of these may travel a little way underground. Other little plants begin to grow from this second root.

Some plants, such as the strawberry, send out stems on top of the ground. These stems make roots where they touch the ground. They start other plants.

This plant sends out a long leaf that takes root. It is called a **walking fern** because it grows step by step, leaf by leaf.

Plants from Underground Stems

Some plants have thick underground stems. The thick stems store food for the plant.

Iris

Cattails

These underground stems send out roots to make new plants. We can cut these underground stems where they form new roots. We can plant each little piece in its own bit of soil. In this way we can get new plants.

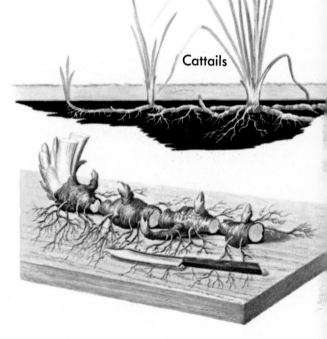

TRY THIS

The white potato that you eat is another kind of thick underground stem. If you cut a potato into pieces, each piece will grow into a potato plant. Each piece must have an "eye" in it.

Try growing a potato. It is easy, especially in spring.

Plants from Bulbs

There are other plants that store food. They do it with little onionlike growths we call **bulbs**. You can easily see for yourself how a bulb grows into a new plant.

FIND OUT

An onion is a bulb. Cut open an onion. The inside is really a group of short, thick leaves, very close together.

If you set a whole onion in water, new roots will grow down and leaves will grow up. Have you ever seen onion bulbs begin to grow this way at home?

Problem

Here are some plants that grow from bulbs. Can you find out what they are?

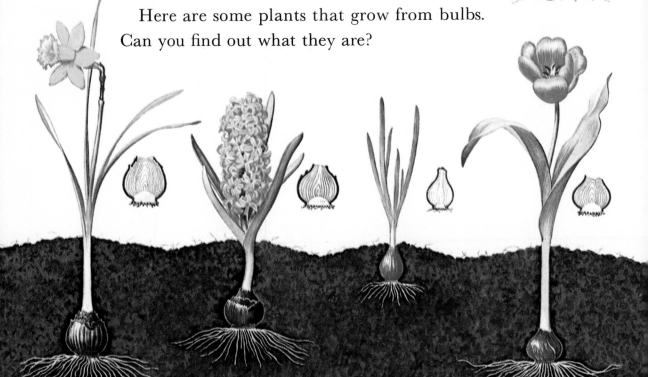

Plants from Roots

A sweet potato is the thick root of a sweet potato plant. Plants store food in these roots during the summer. In the next summer these roots can sprout new stems and leaves and roots. In this way just one plant will become many plants.

TRY THIS

You can see a sweet potato begin to grow into a new plant. Put a firm, bumpy sweet potato into a jar of water. Put the pointed end down, and pour in enough water to cover half the sweet potato.

Put the sweet potato in a warm, dark place. Look at it every few days. When you can see stems and roots beginning to push out, you may set the sweet potato in the sunlight.

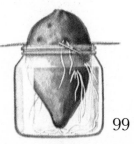

Plants from Cuttings

Many kinds of plant stems can be cut into pieces to make more plants. The pieces or cuttings are planted in damp sand or soil or water to get their roots started. A new plant grows from each cutting. Gardeners get new plants from these parent plants.

Trees

A tree is a plant like all the other plants you have studied. It has leaves and stems and roots. But it is a very big plant. Most trees grow from seeds.

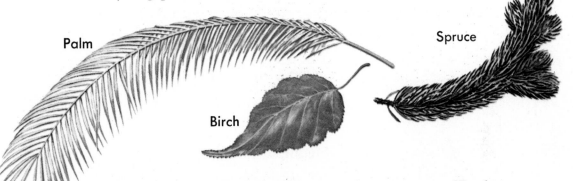

Palm

Spruce

Birch

The leaves make the food that the tree uses. To do this, the leaves must have sunlight. They need water and minerals, too.

Palm

Birch

Spruce

Each kind of tree has a different kind of bark. Bark is a covering that protects the inside of the tree from insects and other animals that might eat it. Bark also protects the tree just as wax paper protects a moist sandwich. It keeps the inside of the tree from drying out.

The water and minerals that a tree needs come into the tree through the roots.

Spruce

You know that minerals and water go through tubes to the leaves. You can see this in a twig.

TRY THIS

You will need two freshly cut twigs with leaves on them, two glass jars, water, and some red ink.

Put one twig in a jar with some red ink, and the other in a jar with some water. Let them stand overnight.

What do you observe? Do you find new red or dark-brown lines in the leaves of one of the twigs? How far up did the red ink flow?

The next day cut the colored twig down the middle. Do you see that part of the twig is red all the way from bottom to top?

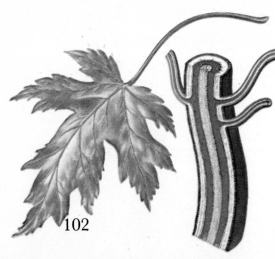

In the red lines of the leaves and twig are tiny end-to-end tubes. Trees have millions of tubes. Water and minerals from the soil travel from the roots to the leaves in these tiny tubes.

102

When new leaves are formed, new tubes are made in the twig. The new tubes are made just inside the bark. Along with the tubes, wood fibers grow. The wood fibers make the tree strong.

Every year a new layer of tubes and fibers grows around the tubes and fibers of the year before. That is why a cut tree looks like this. Each layer is one year's growth of tubes and fibers.

These layers are the wood of a tree. You know how these are useful to the tree. Do you know how they are useful to you? In pencils, tables, chairs—in everything made of wood—there are thousands of tree tubes and fibers.

549

800

1066

1492

1620

1933

California Redwood

Even the paper of this book is made of tubes and fibers. You can see them by tearing a bit of newspaper. Hold it near a light and look at the torn edge with a strong magnifying lens.

Useful Products from Trees

Can you name ten things in your classroom which come from trees?

English Walnut

Grapefruit

Cork Tree

Longleaf Pine

Cascara Tree

Rubber Tree

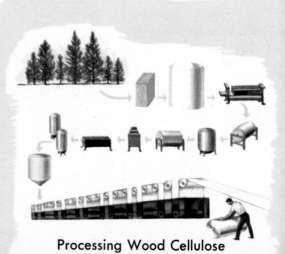

Processing Wood Cellulose

Sugar from Trees

Farmers make maple syrup and maple sugar from the sap of the maple tree. Sap is a watery liquid with a little sugar in it.

Early in the spring the trees are full of sap. The sugar will be food for the young leaves that will open in warm weather. Sugar-maple trees make so much sap that we can take some of it and still leave enough for the young leaves.

To get the sap, a hole is drilled in the trunk of the tree. The sap drips out, a drop at a time, into a bucket. How can the sugar in the sap be taken out?

What happens to water when it is heated? If part of the water is evaporated by heating the sap, maple syrup is left. If almost all the water is evaporated, we get delicious light-brown maple sugar.

Hard and Soft Wood

Different kinds of trees make different kinds of wood. If you have worked with wood, you know that some kinds are harder to cut than others. You can test wood for hardness.

Scientists use a special hardness-testing machine. You can make one almost like it.

EXPERIMENT

You will need a hammer, a piece of string, some different kinds of wood, and a small steel ball.

Put the steel ball on some soft wood. Hold the hammer like this and let it drop. When the hammer hits the ball, it will drive the ball a little way into the wood. Keep on lifting and dropping the hammer until the ball is driven halfway into the wood.

Now test other kinds of wood. How many blows of the hammer did you need for each kind of wood? Keep a record. Which wood was hardest? Which was softest? Were you able to drive the steel ball into every kind of wood?

KIND OF WOOD	NUMBER OF HITS
OAK	
PINE	
MAPLE	
HICKORY	
SPRUCE	
ASH	

Some Hard Woods and Their Uses

Red Oak

Mahogany

Circassian Walnut

Some Soft Woods and Their Uses

White Pine

Douglas Fir

Southern Pine

Talk about the different kinds of wood used above.

Try to find some of these to test for hardness.

Douglas Fir

California Redwood

Tamarack

Hemlock

White Pine

White Spruce

Collect wood samples from these trees. Most of them
stay green all year. Are they hardwoods or softwoods?

108

Silver Maple

White Oak

Aspen

Wild Cherry

Red Ash

American Elm

Most of these trees lose their leaves in the winter.
Find out whether they are hardwoods or softwoods.

Common Coconut Palm

Washington Palm

Cabbage Palmetto

Date Palm

Royal Palm

Yucca or Joshua Tree

Do trees like this grow where you live? Do you think their wood would be hard or soft?

Animals Depend on Plants

You know that all animals depend on plants to live. Some animals eat plants. Some animals eat animals that eat plants.

In a forest there are many, many animals. Some get their food from the plants in the forest. Some get their food by eating smaller animals.

Female Virginia Deer

Gray Fox

Cottontail Rabbit

Problem

What is the food of each animal in the picture?

Does it eat both plants and animals?

If the forest were cut down, how would each animal's life be different?

111

Towhee

Squirrel

OBSERVE AND FIND OUT

1. Find six different kinds of trees. Tell about the shape, bark, and leaves of each one.

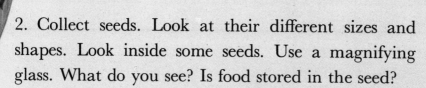

2. Collect seeds. Look at their different sizes and shapes. Look inside some seeds. Use a magnifying glass. What do you see? Is food stored in the seed?

Sort the seeds into piles according to the way they are scattered. Make a chart like the one below.

HOW SEEDS ARE SCATTERED			
WIND	WATER	ANIMALS	GRAVITY

EXPLORE AND FIND OUT

Take a trip to the market.

1. Find out about nuts we eat. Find out from which tree each kind of nut grows. In what way do nuts help mammals and birds?

2. Look for plants you eat. Make a list of the ones you find. Which ones are roots? Which are stems? Which are mainly leaves?

FIND OUT THROUGH EXPERIMENTS

1. Get some bare-looking soil from a nearby lot. Place it in a pot. Do not add seeds. Just water it to keep it from drying out. Does anything happen? Keep a record.

2. Plant 20 radish seeds. Water them daily. How many seeds begin to grow? After the seeds begin to grow, pull up one plant each day. Rinse the roots. Make a picture each day.

3. Why are there so many dandelions growing? How do dandelions spoil people's lawns?

    a. Find a dandelion in some grass. Lift up the leaves. Does grass grow underneath?

    b. Try to dig up a dandelion and its whole root. Measure the root. Is it difficult to pull a dandelion out of the soil? Is it like most roots you have seen?
       How is it different?

    c. What are dandelion seeds like? What scatters these seeds? Plant some dandelion seeds in a pot or outdoors. Watch how they grow.

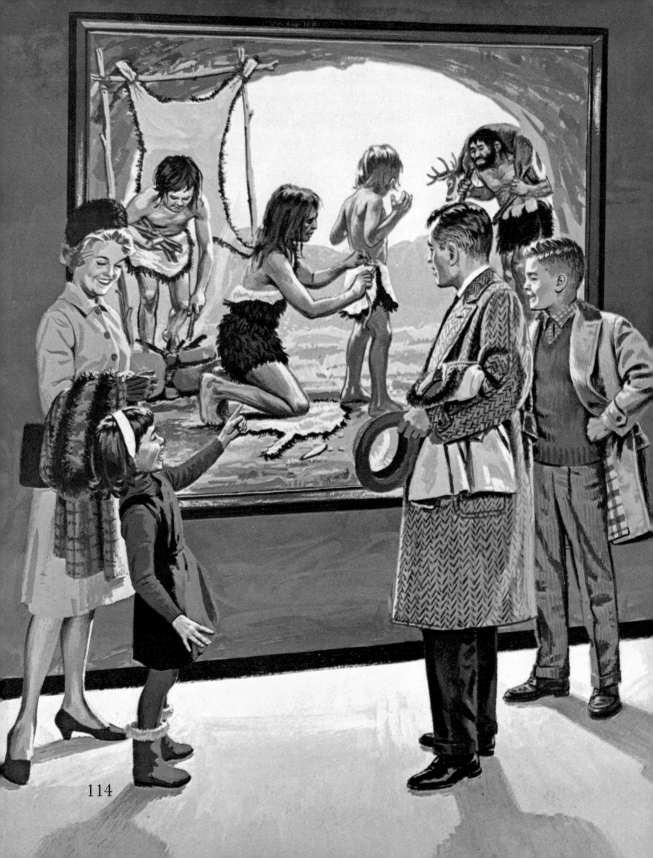

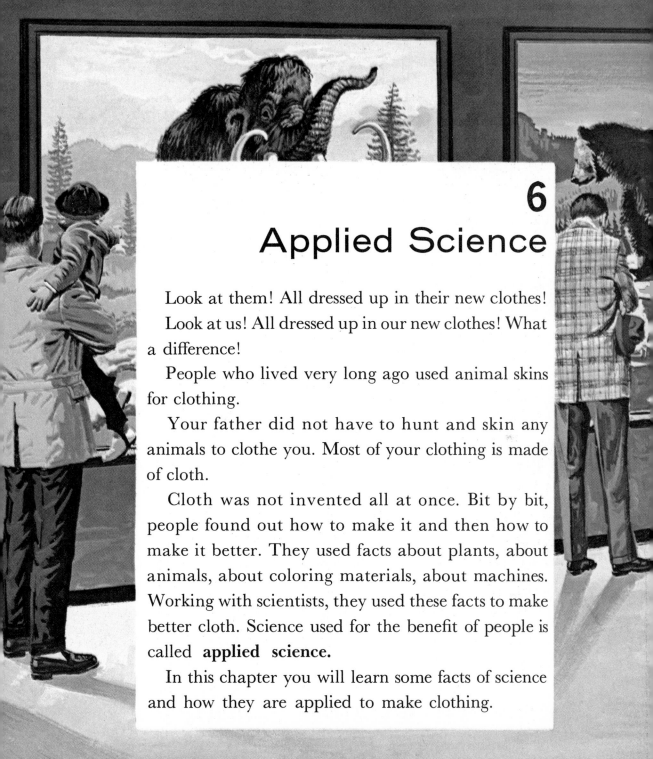

6
Applied Science

Look at them! All dressed up in their new clothes!

Look at us! All dressed up in our new clothes! What a difference!

People who lived very long ago used animal skins for clothing.

Your father did not have to hunt and skin any animals to clothe you. Most of your clothing is made of cloth.

Cloth was not invented all at once. Bit by bit, people found out how to make it and then how to make it better. They used facts about plants, about animals, about coloring materials, about machines. Working with scientists, they used these facts to make better cloth. Science used for the benefit of people is called **applied science.**

In this chapter you will learn some facts of science and how they are applied to make clothing.

OBSERVE

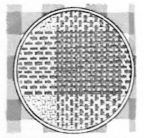

Bring some small pieces of cloth to school. Observe the different pieces. What can you tell about them? You may wish to use some of these words: *smooth, rough, hard, soft, shiny, dull, thick, thin.*

Of course you will want to use words about color. Is there a pattern on the cloth? Is the pattern made by the color on top of the cloth, like a painting? Or does each thread have its own color?

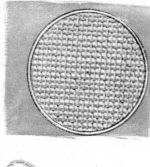

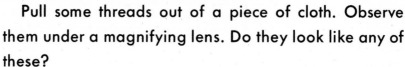

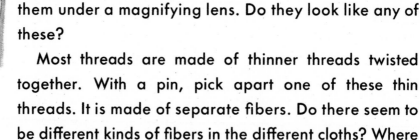

Pull some threads out of a piece of cloth. Observe them under a magnifying lens. Do they look like any of these?

Most threads are made of thinner threads twisted together. With a pin, pick apart one of these thin threads. It is made of separate fibers. Do there seem to be different kinds of fibers in the different cloths? Where do fibers come from?

116

Mammals Have Hair

You can easily find some fibers. Put your hand to your hair. Some hair is straight. Some is curly. But all of it is fiber. Hair is a fiber.

Hair may be any one of many colors. The colors come from substances called **pigments**. Different pigments give color to hair. Other pigments give color to skin and eyes. Everyone has pigments. Some people have more pigments than others.

Many animals grow hair. Such animals are called mammals. In the picture you can see some mammals getting their hair cut.

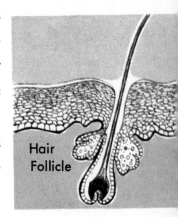

Hair
Follicle

There are many kinds of mammals in many different shapes, sizes, and colors. But they all grow hair.

The hair of some mammals is called fur. The hair of others is wool. Animals have been raised for their wool for thousands of years. Scientists have studied ways of raising animals that grow thicker and longer wool. Scientists who study about all living things are called **biologists.**

Some biologists study ways of improving animals that furnish fibers for cloth. The fur or hair of the animals pictured on page 119 is used for making cloth. Find out more about each animal.

Can you see some ways in which different kinds of biologists could have helped improve wool?

Look at the sheep on this page. Which do you think gives thicker wool?

118

Bactrian Camel

Alpaca

Merino Sheep

Angora Goat

119

Angora Rabbit

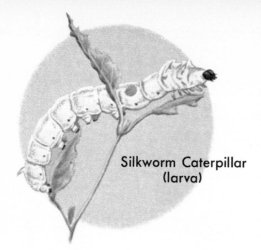
Silkworm Caterpillar
(larva)

Thread from Insects

Some other animals make fibers, too. Here is a caterpillar beginning to spin a covering of silk fiber.

The silk covering is its cocoon. In its cocoon, the caterpillar changes to a pupa. The pupa lies quiet for two weeks.

Larva

Cocoon

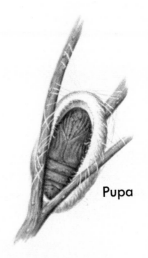
Pupa

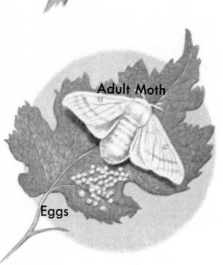
Adult Moth

Eggs

Then it becomes a moth and comes out of the cocoon. The moth flies about. It lays its eggs.

Caterpillars hatch from these eggs. They make their cocoons. Then what happens?

From caterpillar to pupa to moth to eggs, over and over. This is the life cycle of moths.

120

Silkworms and Silk

Many kinds of caterpillars make cocoons of fibers. One kind makes silk fibers that are very good for making soft, smooth cloth. This kind of caterpillar is called a **silkworm.**

The people of China found out how to raise silkworms and to make silk cloth more than three thousand years ago.

They learned how to unwind silk fibers from the silkworm cocoons. They twisted the silk fibers into thread. The thread was used to make fine silk cloth.

At one time silkworms were almost all killed by a disease. But a biologist named Pasteur discovered a cure.

Problem

Find out what Louis Pasteur did. Find out how the silkworm was saved through applied science.

Fibers in Plants

We also get fibers from plants. Here is a way to look at some plant fibers.

TRY THIS

You will need a stalk of fresh celery, two glasses, red ink, a magnifying lens, and water.

Cut off the end of the celery stalk. Split the stalk as in the picture. Put half of the stalk into red ink. Put the other half into water. Let it stand for one day.

Next day observe the stalk in the water with a magnifying lens. The lines are thin tubes and fibers. Pull away some of the fibers. Look at the leaves. What do you see?

Now examine the stalk of celery in the red ink. Cut through the stalk. Look at the end. Is there red ink in the stalk?

Here is how you can see other plant fibers. Get some stems and stalks from several different kinds of plants. Pull them apart the long way. You will find fibers in almost every plant.

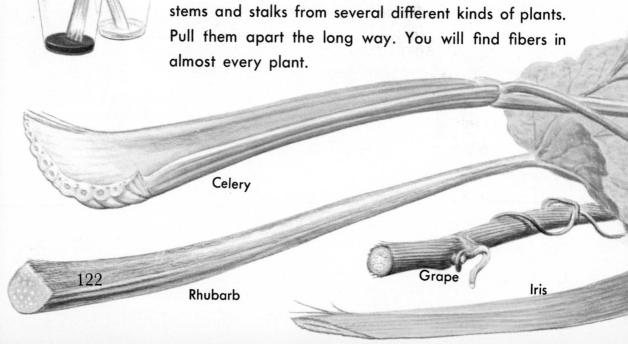

Celery

Rhubarb

Grape

Iris

We Use Plant Fibers

All over the world people have learned to use plant fibers to make many things. Here are some examples.

Jute

Flax

Cotton

Sisal Hemp

Manila Hemp

Thread from Cotton

One of the most important cloths is cotton cloth.

Look at the picture. Number 1 shows a cotton bush, a leaf, and a flower.

As the flower ripens, the petals fall off. The base of the flower is a seed pod (number 2). It grows and pops open. Each seed has many fluffy white cotton fibers (number 3).

The seeds are combed out by a machine that looks like a round comb with many teeth. Such a machine is a cotton gin. Before the cotton gin, the seeds were picked out by hand. It took one person a day to pick the seeds from a pound of cotton!

TRY THIS

Take a piece of fluffy cotton.

Pull away a little bit and begin twisting it into a thread. Keep pulling and twisting, to see how thin and smooth a thread you can spin. How long does it take to make one foot of thin, smooth thread?

Machines to Spin Thread

Fingers spin thread slowly. Is there any way of spinning thread faster? You can find out.

EXPERIMENT

You will need a board, two nails, a ribbon spool, a thread spool, a hammer, a long rubber band, a pencil.

Put them together like this:

 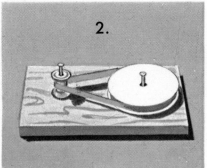 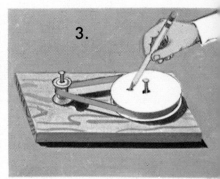

Use the pencil to turn the ribbon spool. Make one full turn. Count the turns of the thread spool.

The ribbon spool is like a big wheel. What is like a small wheel? The big wheel turns the small wheel. Is this a way to change a slow spin into a fast one?

Here is a spinning wheel. Find the large wheel. What turns it? Find a small wheel. What turns it? What does the small wheel do?

Long ago people found out about wheels. Then wheels were used in a spinning wheel. The people applied science to make work easier.

Weaving on Looms

After the thread is spun, it is made into cloth. This is called **weaving**.

Weaving is done on a machine called a **loom.** In the picture above, a hand loom is being used to weave a blanket. Find the long threads going up and down. The woman is pulling another thread across. She pulls it under one long thread and over the next.

You can see the same under-and-over weaving in cloth or burlap woven on a power machine.

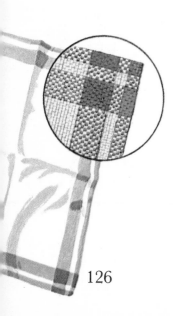

A power loom works much faster than a handloom. One worker can tend many power looms. Cloth woven this way costs much less than hand-woven cloth.

Automated Machines

Now we have power looms that are still better. These looms run themselves. A machine that runs itself is called an **automated machine**. *Automated* means "by itself."

An automated loom is really two kinds of machines. A power loom weaves the cloth. Other machines run the power loom. If a thread breaks, they stop the loom, tie a knot, and start it again. They can measure, pack, weigh, and load the cloth. One worker can take care of many automated looms.

Color for Cloth

The colors on cloth are made with dyes. The first dyes were made from plants. Some dyes are still made from plants. You can make some dyes yourself.

FIND OUT

Get some cut vegetables and two pans with water. Soak chopped spinach in one pan. Soak cut beets in another. Put two small pieces of white cloth in each pan. Take out the cloths the next day and let them dry. What do you see? Now wash one cloth of each color. Hold them next to the unwashed cloths. What has happened to the colors?

Long ago somebody tried boiling cloth in the dye. Plan an experiment to see if this is a better way.

Today most dyes do not come from plants. They are made of other substances, such as coal tar.

All these bright rainbow colors are made from black, sticky coal tar!

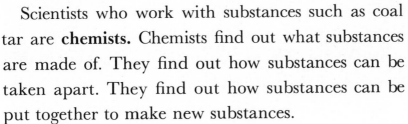

Scientists who work with substances such as coal tar are **chemists.** Chemists find out what substances are made of. They find out how substances can be taken apart. They find out how substances can be put together to make new substances.

Chemists can make many kinds of dyes and coloring materials. They can make dyes of any color, dyes that do not fade, dyes you can eat, dyes that can color Easter eggs. And they know how to make these dyes so that they do not cost very much.

Problem

Make a list of colors you see in cloth in one day.

Make a list of different things you use that are dyed.

Spinneret

Chemists Make New Fibers

Chemists have taken substances apart and put them together to make new fibers. They make the new fibers out of wood, straw, coal, sand—even out of milk and beans.

One kind of fiber made by chemists is **rayon**. Most rayon is made from wood.

Small pieces of wood are mixed with other substances and boiled. These substances change the wood until it is as soft as cooked cereal. Then it is squeezed out through tiny holes. It comes out in thin fibers which are later hardened.

Another kind of fiber is made from milk. You can try making it. It's not much of a fiber, but you will see how a liquid can be changed to a soft solid.

EXPERIMENT

You will need a little milk, a glass of vinegar, and an eyedropper.

Fill the eyedropper with milk. Hold the open end in the vinegar. Empty it slowly. You will see the milk become a thick, soft thread.

In a factory the milk is squeezed out of very small holes into a liquid such as vinegar.

Many other things are done to the fibers before they are ready to be woven into cloth.

Chemists have used science for making new kinds of cloth. You may be wearing a fur-lined coat that was made from coal!

TRY THIS

Collect clothing labels that give the names of the fibers in the clothing. Put them on a chart and see what you can find out about each fiber. How will you group the labels?

Some labels will tell about cloth made from plant or animal fibers. How did scientists help? Some new fibers came from experiments. Which scientists helped?

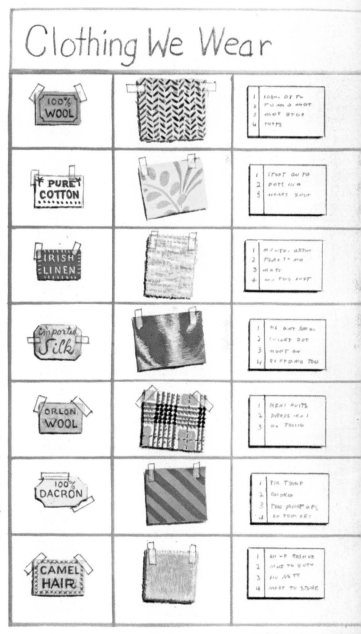

Clothing We Wear

Plastics for Clothing

You found out that some soft substances can be made into fibers. These substances are called plastics. Plastics can be made into other shapes, too.

Suppose the soft plastic is squeezed out of a narrow slot like this. What do we have when it hardens? A ribbon!

Suppose a narrow plastic ribbon is bent into a curly shape like this. What do we have? A plastic zipper!

Suppose the plastic is poured into a space like this. When it hardens, what comes out? A button!

Suppose we dip this shape into liquid plastic. Then we take it out, with wet plastic on it. When the plastic hardens, we can peel off a glove!

What plastic clothing do you have in your home? Make a list.

132

You can make a little plastic rain hat.

TRY THIS

You will need modeling clay and nail polish.
Nail polish is one kind of plastic.

Make the clay into a shape like this.

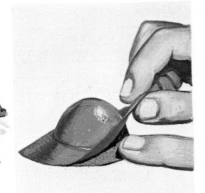

Paint it with nail polish. When it is dry, paint it again.
Do this three times. Then carefully peel away the hardened nail polish. You have made a little plastic hat!

Just think of the many different kinds of clothing
you have. Think of the plastic fibers, and the fibers
from plants and animals. Think of the dyes, and the
spinning and weaving machines. Because of applied
science, you have more and better clothing than the
people of long ago did.

OBSERVE AND FIND OUT

1. Look at the different materials of which the clothes you are wearing are made. What are some of the differences in color, thickness, and the way the different kinds of material feel? Use such words as *soft, smooth, slippery, rough,* and *elastic.*

2. Make a chart like the one below about the clothes you are wearing. Be sure to list all your clothes.

CLOTHING	WHAT IS IT MADE OF	SOURCE				
		PLANT	MAMMAL	REPTILE	INSECT	MAN-MADE
shoes	leather		cow			

3. Try to find a cocoon. Take it apart carefully. What is it made of? What is inside?

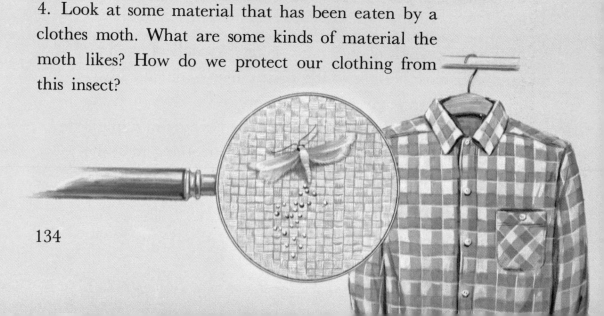

4. Look at some material that has been eaten by a clothes moth. What are some kinds of material the moth likes? How do we protect our clothing from this insect?

FIND OUT FROM BOOKS

1. Find out about some plants that are used to make cloth or rope. What does man make from the cloth or rope you found out about?

2. Find out about some insects and spiders that spin threads. How are the threads useful to the insects? Are the insects harmful or useful to man?

3. Spiders are not insects. What differences can you see between the spider and insect pictured here? Find out what other differences there are.

DO THIS AND FIND OUT

1. Untwist the fibers from a 6-inch piece of knitting yarn. Spin a long piece of yarn by twisting together the short fibers. What makes these wool fibers stay together? Look at the fibers under a magnifying glass. Pull on the end of a fiber and let go. What can you tell about this animal fiber?

2. Man-made fibers are used to make many kinds of cloth. Make a collection of bits of this cloth. Put them on a chart. Tell what they are made of.

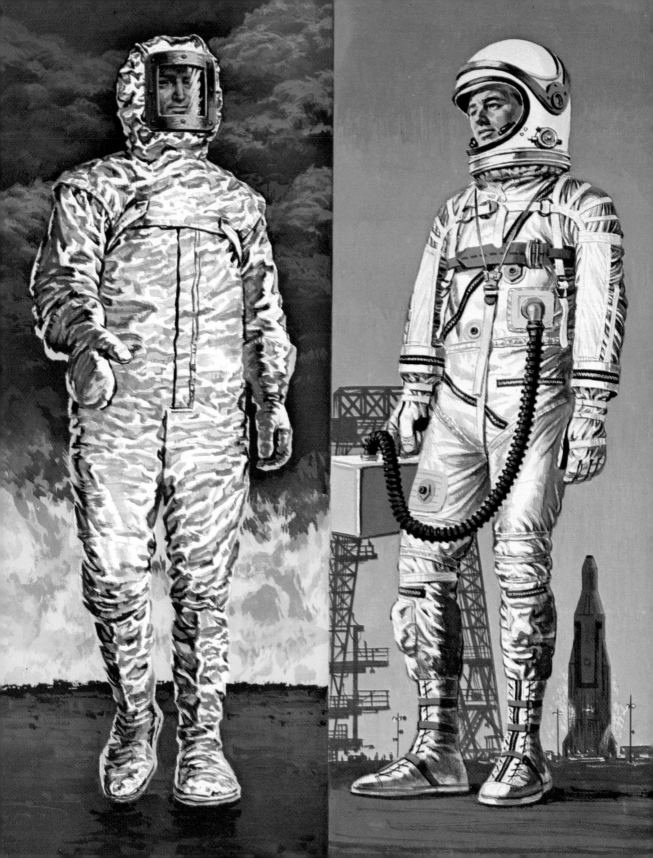

7
Heat

These explorers are dressed in three strange suits. Which explorer is dressed to keep warm? To keep cool? Which explorer is wearing clothing that can do both—keep him warm in cold weather and cool in hot weather?

Your clothes are not as strange as the explorers'. But you, too, have to think about being warm or cold. Some materials keep heat in. Some keep heat out.

In buildings, too, we want materials that do these things. When do we want to keep heat in? When would we like to keep heat out?

Let's find out about keeping heat in and out.

Insulation

Fur or wool keeps you warm. How? These experiments help you think about the answer.

EXPERIMENT

1. You will need two glass jars with covers, a piece of fur or wool, hot water, and ice cubes.

Fill the two jars with hot water. Wrap one in fur or wool. Let both jars stand. What do you think will happen? Why? Check your guess with a thermometer.

Do you think the fur or wool put heat into the water?

The next part of the experiment will help you find out.

2. Put three ice cubes and cold water in each jar. Wrap one in fur or wool. Put both jars in a warm place.

What do you think will happen? Why? Try it and see.

The ice cubes melt when heat comes in.

The hot water cools when heat goes out.

Do fur and wool keep heat from coming in? From going out?

A material that keeps heat from passing through is called a **heat insulator.** There are many different materials used as heat insulators.

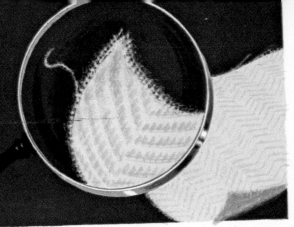

How does an insulator keep heat from passing through? If you look closely at wool, you can see many fibers. But there is something else that you cannot see. Here is a way to find out what it is.

TRY THIS

You will need a piece of fur or wool, a pencil, and a glass of water.

Put a piece of fur or wool in a glass of water. Push it down with a pencil. Look at the air bubbles.

Wool, fur, and other fluffy materials have lots of air trapped among the fibers.

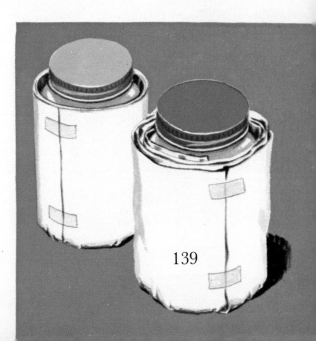

Scientists say that heat does not go easily through air. They say that air is a poor conductor of heat.

Find out for yourself if air is a poor conductor.

EXPERIMENT

Fill two jars with hot water. Put the cover of each jar on tightly. Next, wrap one jar loosely with paper, leaving plenty of air spaces. Wrap the other jar tightly with paper. Leave both jars for half an hour. Then remove the covers. In which jar is the water warmer?

139

Poor Conductors

Trapped air does not conduct heat quickly. This fact can be useful, as pictured below.

A potholder is an insulator. It is made of fluffy cloth. Where is the trapped air? Which way does it keep heat from being conducted?

Refrigerators are lined with fluffy material. Explain why this is good insulation.

Here is insulation being put under a roof. How does this insulate in summer? How does it insulate in winter?

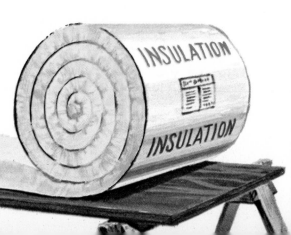

Good Conductors

If a pot did not let heat in, could you cook with it? Sometimes we want a good conductor.

You can find some substances which are good conductors. Guess whether each one is a good conductor and then test your guess.

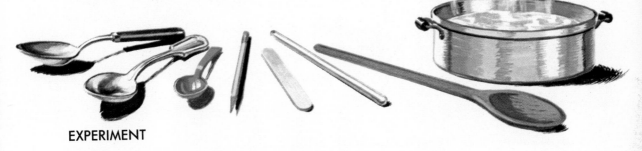

EXPERIMENT

You will need a pencil, a silver spoon, a stainless-steel spoon, a plastic spoon, a soda straw, and a pan of hot water.

One at a time, hold each of the things to be tested in a pan of hot water. Your fingers will tell you which ones conduct heat quickly. Which ones do not?

The hot water should be kept hot all through the experiment. Why?

If you look at dry wood through a strong magnifying lens, the wood looks like this. Can you see little box shapes? They are filled with air. How does this explain the pencil part of the experiment?

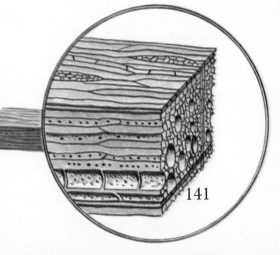

141

Heat from Rays

How does a fire make you warm? The fire does not touch you, yet you feel the heat. Can it be that the fire heats the air and then the air heats you? You can find out with the heat from an electric light bulb.

EXPERIMENT

You will need a clear glass bowl and a lamp.

Put the clear glass bowl around a large electric light bulb. Hold your hand near it. Turn on the light. Do you feel heat? How do you know the heat does not come from heated air?

142

All hot things give off heat rays. You cannot see the rays. They do not heat air or glass. But they heat many other things.

That is how the sun's heat reaches you. It comes in rays. In some ways they are like light rays. They are reflected by shiny things.

Can you tell what this experiment is about? What do you think may happen? Why? Try it and see.

Look at the picture on pages 136–137. One of the men is wearing a shiny suit. Can you tell why?

Fire

This is not the easiest way to start a fire. A match is quicker. But before there were matches people had other ways of starting fires.

Back and forth, back and forth, the string spins the stick. The spinning point rubs against the block of wood. The point becomes very hot. It sets fire to bits of dry grass on the wood.

To have a fire we need a substance to burn. This is called a fuel. What are some fuels? To start the fuel burning we need heat. And we need something else. Can you tell what that is from the next experiment?

EXPERIMENT

Air is a mixture of gases.

The gas needed for burning is oxygen.

About one fifth of the air is oxygen.

Put a jar over a burning candle. What do you think will happen? Try it and see.

Does this seem to show that air is needed to keep a fuel burning?

It seems so, but we can't be sure. Now try the experiment illustrated below. Why should this second experiment give you a better answer to the question above?

145

Problem

Can you answer these questions about each of the fires in the pictures?

What is the fuel?

How does oxygen get to the fire?

What heat starts the fire?

Do we use the fire for heat or light?

146

Fire Safety

All the rules about safety with fire are rules about fuel, oxygen, and heat. Bring these three together and you have a fire. Take away any one, and the fire goes out.

Problem

Here are some fire-safety rules. In each safety rule one thing is taken away. What is it?

1. Pour sand over a campfire when you are through using it.

2. Do not keep paper or other things that can burn easily near a furnace.

3. If a person's clothes are on fire, wrap him in a wool blanket or rug.

Find out about more fire-safety rules in your school and town. How does each rule help?

Heating Rooms

It's fun to sit in front of a campfire and warm yourself. Nobody sits in front of this fire, and yet it warms many people in many rooms of a school building.

This fire is burning in a furnace. The furnace is in the cellar of a school building.

What fuel is being burned? Is it the same fuel as that burned in your school? Are there special ways for letting in air?

Have you ever watched a kettle of boiling water? Does the steam go down or up?

In a furnace, fire heats water and turns it to steam. The fuel for the fire may be coal, gas, or oil. The hot steam pushes its way through pipes that go up to the classrooms.

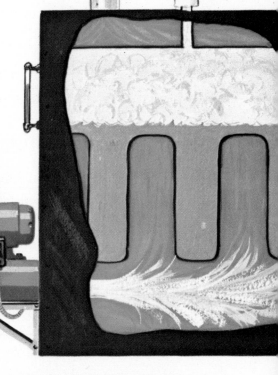

UNDERGROUND
FUEL TANK

The pipes are joined to radiators. The steam from the pipes flows into the radiators and makes them hot. That is how a fire in the cellar can send heat to rooms up above. The heat is carried by the steam. Does steam carry the heat in your school?

A radiator is at one side of the room. How does the rest of the room become warm? You can find out with two chalkboard erasers.

TRY THIS

Hold two chalkboard erasers over a hot radiator or an electric lamp.

Clap the erasers together to make the chalk dust fly.

You will see the chalk dust move in the air. Do you see the chalk dust moving up over the hot radiator or the lamp?

The chalk dust moves up because the air is moving up. When air is heated, it moves up. It is pushed up from underneath by cool air.

If you could follow the moving air, you would see it flow up higher in the room and then move across to other parts of the room. The warm air warms the things along the way.

Now hold the erasers under the warm radiator or the lamp. Clap them together again.

Do you see chalk dust moving toward the warm radiator or the lamp? The chalk dust is being carried by cool air moving in.

Near a warm radiator there is cool air moving in. It is warmed when it touches the warm radiator. Then it moves up and out into the room.

Over and over again, the air keeps going in a circle around the room. It gives its heat to the things in the room and then comes back to the radiator again. In this way the radiator can heat the whole room.

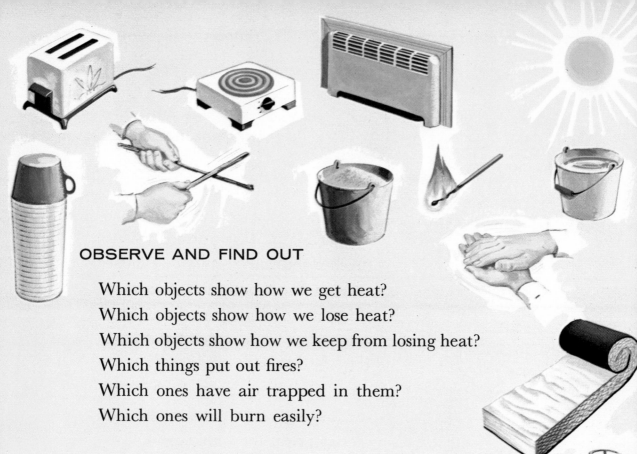

OBSERVE AND FIND OUT

Which objects show how we get heat?

Which objects show how we lose heat?

Which objects show how we keep from losing heat?

Which things put out fires?

Which ones have air trapped in them?

Which ones will burn easily?

FIND OUT FROM OTHERS

1. Plan a trip to the firehouse. Find out some ways in which firemen fight fires. How does water help firemen fight fires? What else do firemen use to fight fires?

2. The custodian might be able to take you on a trip to the furnace room. What fuel is used in the furnace? How does the heat travel to your classroom? How does it travel in the classroom? Find out how your home or apartment building is heated. Compare your home furnace with the school furnace. What is done at your school to prevent fire?

FIND OUT THROUGH EXPERIMENTS

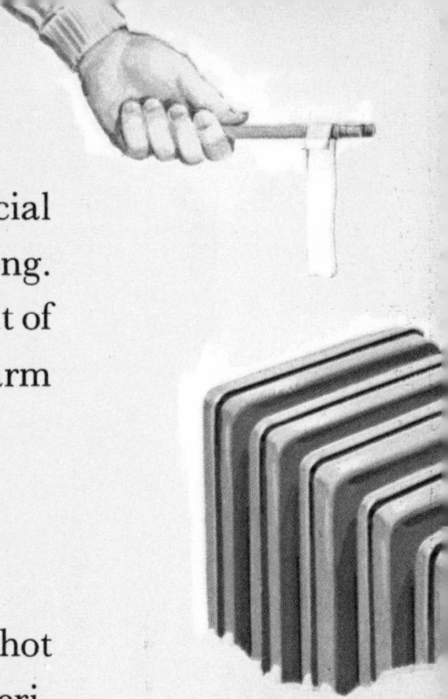

1. Cut a piece of tissue paper or a single sheet of facial tissue into a strip about 1 inch wide and 3 inches long. Attach it to the eraser end of a pencil with a tiny bit of cellophane tape. Hold the pencil over a warm radiator. What happens? Why?

2. Is a light or dark color better on a house in a hot country? How could you find out from the experiment shown here? Fill both tin cans with ice cubes and place them on a sunny windowsill.

DO THIS AND FIND OUT

1. Make a list of conductors and insulators of heat in your kitchen.

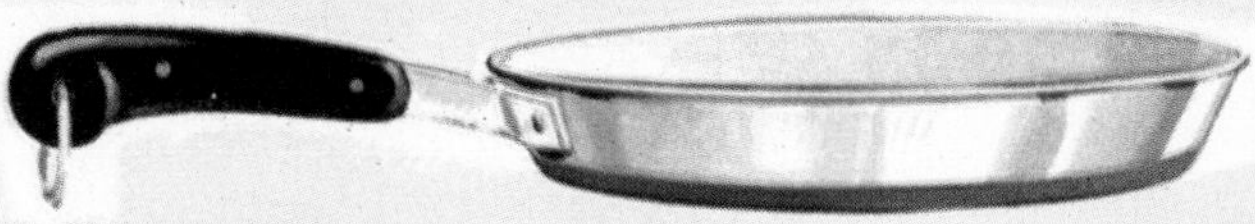

2. Go to a building-materials store. Get some small pieces of heat insulators. Find out how they are used.

153

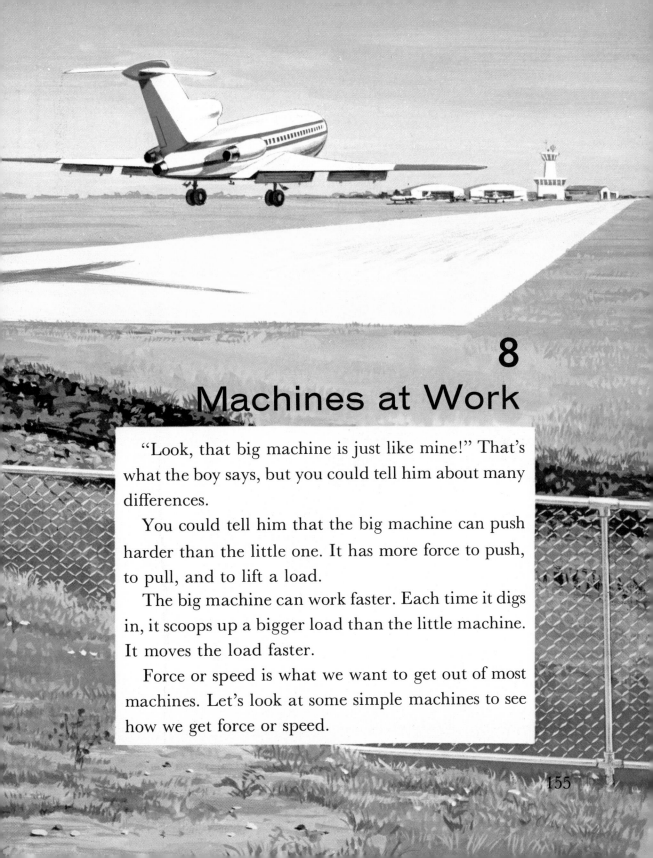

8
Machines at Work

"Look, that big machine is just like mine!" That's what the boy says, but you could tell him about many differences.

You could tell him that the big machine can push harder than the little one. It has more force to push, to pull, and to lift a load.

The big machine can work faster. Each time it digs in, it scoops up a bigger load than the little machine. It moves the load faster.

Force or speed is what we want to get out of most machines. Let's look at some simple machines to see how we get force or speed.

155

Levers

You can't lift a heavy, full-grown man all by yourself. Your muscles don't have enough force. But here's a machine that will increase your force. Try this experiment, as shown in the picture below.

Did your muscles get any stronger? No. But you were able to get more force into the lifting job.

You used the board and block as a machine. Such a machine is called a **lever.** There are many kinds and shapes of levers, but all levers have these parts: (1) The fulcrum, which is the part where the lever turns. The fulcrum itself does not turn. (2) The force arm, which is the part of the lever from the force to the fulcrum. (3) The load arm, which is the part from the fulcrum to the load.

Notice that the fulcrum is near the load. Would it make a difference if you put the fulcrum anywhere else? Try moving the fulcrum to the middle. Can you lift the man? Here is another way of finding out.

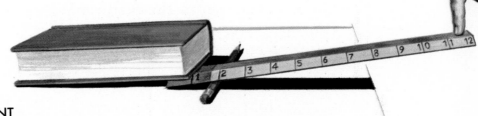

EXPERIMENT

Set up a ruler, pencil, and book like this. The book will be the load to be lifted. What is the force? When the fulcrum is at the 2-inch mark, how long is the force arm? How long is the load arm?

Push down at the 12-inch mark, using one finger. Feel how much force it takes to lift the book. Then move the pencil fulcrum to another place and try again. Here is a way to keep a record of your results.

Fulcrum at	Length of Force Arm	Length of Load Arm	Force Needed
			Very Little
2"	10"	2"	
4"			
6"			157
8"			
10"			

Here is a big stone which must be moved out of the way. It is much too heavy for you to move by the force of your muscles alone. You can use the long iron bar as a lever. You can use the small stone as a fulcrum.

You can put the fulcrum any place you wish. Three places are shown in the picture. Which one would you choose? Why?

Problem

Here's a hard problem for you. Suppose position 1 is one foot from the big stone. Position 2 is two feet away from the big stone. Position 3 is three feet away. The iron bar is six feet long.

When the fulcrum is at position 1, how long is the force arm? How long is the load arm?

Can you answer the same questions when the fulcrum is at position 2? Position 3?

158

Problem

Not all levers are used for lifting heavy loads. What load is being lifted by this lever? Where is the force? The fulcrum? How else is this lever used?

Not all levers are straight. This lever has curved claws for pulling out nails. Nails are not heavy, but much force is needed to pull them out of wood. Where is the fulcrum? Where is the force? What is the load?

Sometimes we use two levers together. These pliers are two levers. In fact, this tool is called a pair of pliers. Pliers are not for lifting or prying. They grip and squeeze the load. Where is the force? The fulcrum?

Find the fulcrum of each lever in the pictures on pages 156–157. In each lever the fulcrum is between the force and the load. Can the fulcrum be somewhere else? Let's see.

EXPERIMENT

You will need a ruler, a string, and a book.

Tie a string around a book. Hang it from a ruler at the 2-inch mark. Lift the end of the ruler with one finger. How heavy does it feel? Move the book to the 4-inch mark, then the 6-, 8-, and 10-inch marks. At which place did you need the least force to lift the book? Did the ruler help you to increase force? Is it a lever? Where is the fulcrum?

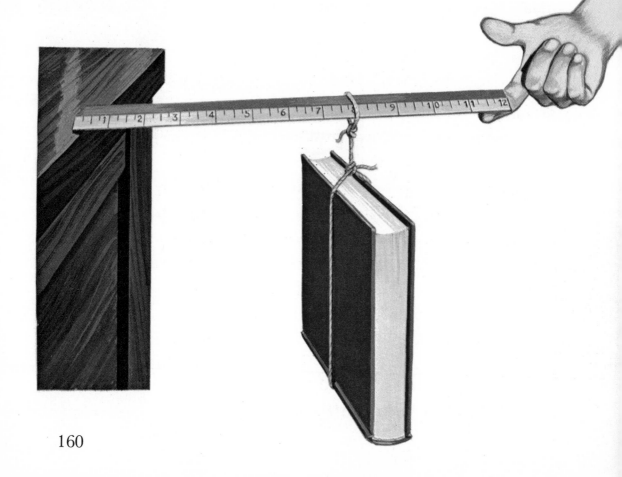

Sometimes we use a lever to increase speed instead of force. Here is a way to see this.

EXPERIMENT

You will need a yardstick.

Hold a yardstick like this. Keep one hand still. (This hand will be the fulcrum.) Move the other hand slowly up and down. Look at the far end of the stick. When your hand moves a short distance, the far end moves a long distance. The far end also moves faster.

This boy is using a lever to move a load quickly. The lever is a fishing rod. The load is a fish. The boy wants to lift the load fast, before it has time to get away. A small move of the boy's hand makes a big, quick move of the far end of the rod.

Where is the force? Where is the fulcrum?

Look at the fishing reel on the rod. It, too, is a machine for increasing speed. After you study the next two pages, try to tell how it works.

161

Faster with Gears

Mixing a cake with a spoon is slow work. An egg beater does the work faster. Wheels make work faster. Let's see how wheels help.

Notice the teeth on the big wheel of a beater. See how they fit into the teeth on the little wheels. The wheels with teeth are gears.

See how the handle turns the big gear. What do the teeth of the big gear push? When the smaller gears turn, what else turns?

Now let's see how this kind of beater saves us work when we want to mix something.

You will need an egg beater.

Make a mark on one of the blades of the beater. Turn the handle slowly.

Count the number of turns the blade makes. How many times does the blade turn while the handle turns just once?

When the big wheel turns once, the little wheel turns many times. Each turn of the handle makes many turns of the blades.

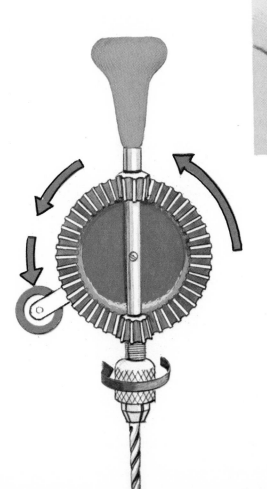

A hand drill, too, has a big gear and a little one.

When a big gear turns a little gear, the work is speeded up.

163

When did you give up three wheels? Now you ride four wheels!

Can you find the four wheels on the new bicycle? There are two big wheels that roll along on the ground. There are also two smaller wheels that do something else. Let's see what they do.

Look at wheel 1 and wheel 2. Notice that both wheels are gears. A chain goes around both gears. The chain fits the teeth of both gears.

When gear 1 is turned, it moves the chain. What does the moving chain do to gear 2?

Gear 2 is really part of the big rear wheel of the bicycle. When gear 2 turns, it makes the whole rear wheel turn, too. As the rear wheel turns, it makes the whole bicycle move.

Now you understand how your feet turn the wheels of your bicycle. But what do you gain by riding on a bicycle instead of walking? Let's find out.

EXPERIMENT

You will need a bicycle.

See how far you can go when you take two long steps on foot. Then take two steps on a bicycle. You do this by starting with one foot at the top. Push your foot all the way down and then all the way up.

How far did you go in two steps on the bicycle? How far did you go in two steps on foot? What helps you go farther and faster on a bicycle than on foot?

Wedges

Here's a fine dry log for the fire, but it is much too thick to catch fire easily. It has to be split into thinner pieces. The strongest man you can think of is not strong enough to tear it apart with his bare hands. His muscles don't have enough force. He needs a machine that increases force.

Here it is. It is an ax. The head of an ax is thin and sharp along one edge. It gets thicker and thicker toward the other edge. This shape is called a **wedge.**

When you use a wedge, your muscles are strong enough to split hard wood. With a wedge you can even split rock and steel! Let's look at the wedge more closely.

166

A wedge really does two things, one after the other. First, the thin, sharp edge makes a thin cut in the wood. Then the thicker part of the wedge spreads the wood apart. Cut and spread, cut and spread. Wedges help you to increase force.

The wedge is such a useful tool that people make it in many sizes and shapes, for cutting many kinds of materials.

What are these wedges used for? Where is the sharp edge of each? Where is the part of the wedge that does the spreading?

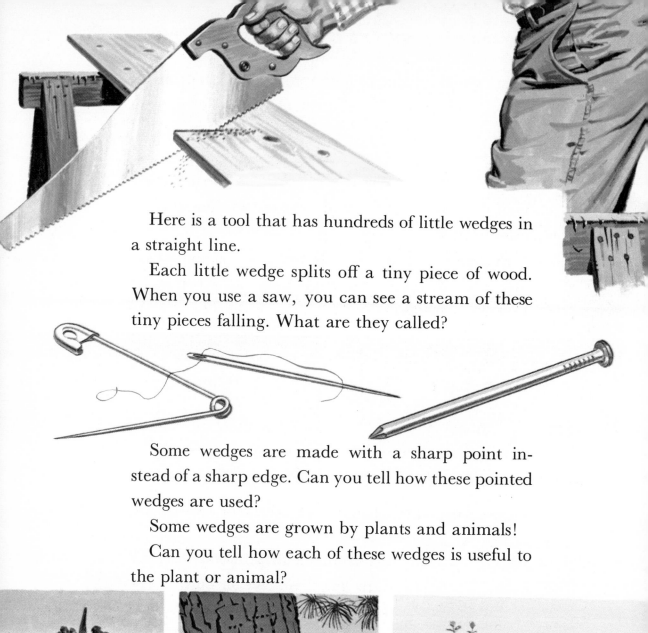

Here is a tool that has hundreds of little wedges in a straight line.

Each little wedge splits off a tiny piece of wood. When you use a saw, you can see a stream of these tiny pieces falling. What are they called?

Some wedges are made with a sharp point instead of a sharp edge. Can you tell how these pointed wedges are used?

Some wedges are grown by plants and animals!

Can you tell how each of these wedges is useful to the plant or animal?

Problem

Look in the store window. Can you find a machine that works like this?

1. A wedge for cutting wood.
2. Many small wedges for cutting wood.
3. Many small wedges for cutting iron.
4. Two levers with one fulcrum, for gripping.
5. Two levers and two wedges, for cutting.
6. A lever for increasing force.
7. A lever for increasing speed.
8. Gears that increase speed.

169

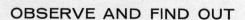

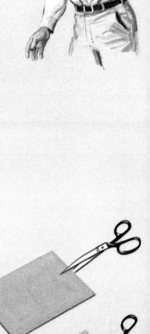

OBSERVE AND FIND OUT

1. How does each of these levers work? Where is the fulcrum in each one? Find other levers on your way to school or at home. Can you tell how each one is used?

2. Puzzle: In your classroom find a machine that has three gears and two sets of wedges. Tell how it works. What is different about the large gear?

3. Puzzle: I am a wedge. I am white. Take good care of me. Brush me twice a day. What am I? How do you use me?

4. Look for all the wedges in your kitchen or in a tool chest. Tell how each one is used.

FIND OUT THROUGH EXPERIMENTS

1. Try to cut a piece of cardboard, using the scissors in two ways: (1) near the tip, (2) near the fulcrum. Can you explain the difference?

2. Balance a ruler on a pencil. Put a paper clip at one end. Where should you put two paper clips to balance it? First guess; then try. Next, put two paper clips at one end. Where will you balance it with two? With three? With four?

170

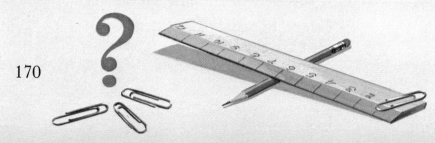

FIND OUT WITH NUMBERS

1. Cut a piece of cardboard into a wedge about 6 inches long. Push this wedge through some sand. Which way does the sand move? Measure how far the sand is pushed to each side. Measure how wide the wedge is. What do you find out about a wedge?

2. The arrow shows which way the large gear turns. Which way does the small gear turn? Each time the large gear turns around once, how many turns will the small gear make? Each time the large gear turns one tooth, how many teeth will the small gear turn?

3. The seesaw is a lever that can balance weights. With the two children in the picture on the seesaw, where must the children sit to balance the seesaw? Move the seesaw to a different fulcrum and balance it. Is it possible to balance it with two children sitting on one end and one child on the other end? Try it.

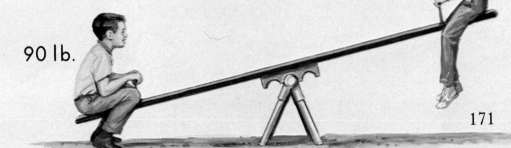

60 lb.

90 lb.

171

172

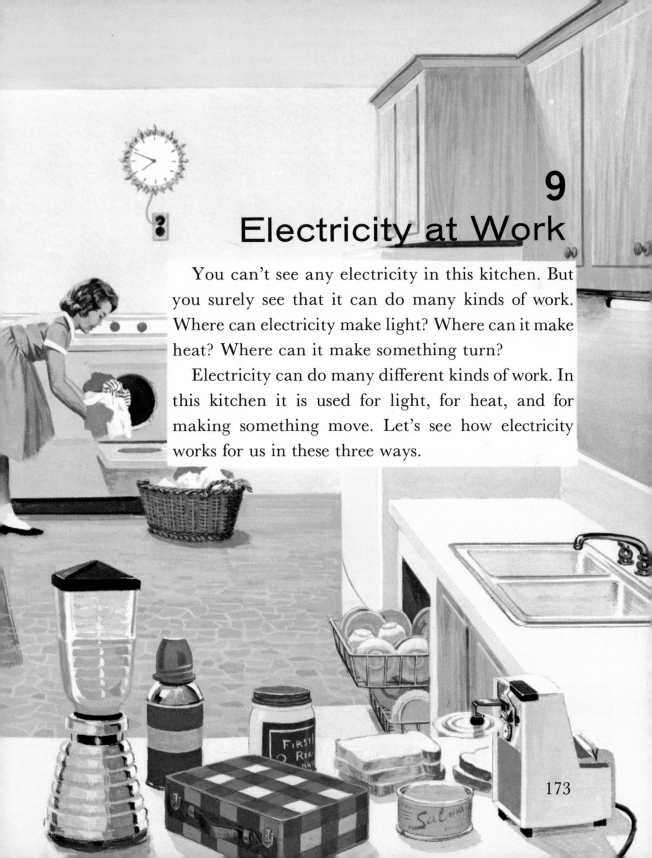

9
Electricity at Work

You can't see any electricity in this kitchen. But you surely see that it can do many kinds of work. Where can electricity make light? Where can it make heat? Where can it make something turn?

Electricity can do many different kinds of work. In this kitchen it is used for light, for heat, and for making something move. Let's see how electricity works for us in these three ways.

Electricity into Light

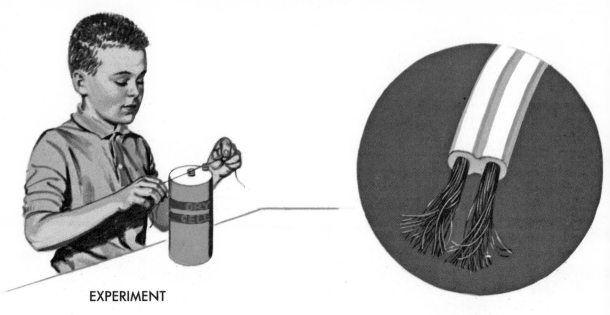

EXPERIMENT

You will need a thin strand of wire and a dry cell. You can get a thin strand of wire from an old piece of electric wire.

First cut away the covering of the wire. This covering is called **insulation.** Then pull out a thin strand of wire about six inches long.

Hold the wire by its two ends and place it across the two screws of the dry cell. These screws are called **terminals.**

Electricity is flowing from one terminal to the other. What do you see happen to the part of the wire between the two terminals?

The electricity from a dry cell is safe to use. But electricity in your house wires can hurt you badly if you try to do experiments with it.

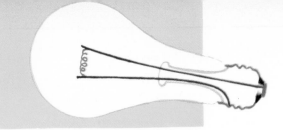

See the thin wire in this electric bulb. It is a **filament.** This word comes from a word meaning hair. Why is this a good name for a thin wire? What happens when electricity flows through the filament?

This electric lamp has no filament. It has a gas that glows when electricity flows through.

Electric lights have many uses. How are all the lights below used?

Electricity into Heat

You have seen that electricity can make the filament in a bulb give off light. The filament also gives off heat, even though we do not want heat from a bulb. But in an electric iron or toaster we want as much heat as possible. How can we get more heat and less light from the electricity?

EXPERIMENT

You will need a thick strand of wire and a dry-cell battery.

Hold the thick strand of wire by its two ends. Place it across the two terminals of the dry cell.

Does it glow as brightly as the thin strand of wire?

Ask somebody to hold a small piece of paper near the wire. Does the paper begin to smoke? It is the heat from the wire that makes the paper so hot.

When enough electricity flows through a wire, we get light and heat. With the same source of electricity, we get more light from a thin wire. We get more heat from a thick wire of the same kind. There are thick wires in electric toasters, heaters, iron, and ranges. You can easily see the wires in electric heaters and toasters.

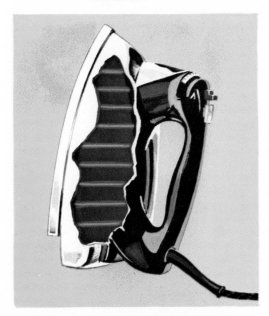

Electricity into Motion

Electricity can move things. Electricity moves the hands of an electric clock. It moves the machinery in a vacuum cleaner, in an electric fan, in an electric train, and in many other things. In your school gong, electricity moves a little hammer that hits the gong and makes it ring. Let's see how electricity can make things move. Let's make a small gong.

EXPERIMENT

You will need a glass jar, some thread, a pencil, a large iron nail, a dry cell, an iron screw or nut, and about five feet of insulated wire.

Wrap the wire around the iron nail, as in the picture.

Cut away the insulation from each end of the wire. Bend each end into a little hook.

Now you have a special kind of magnet called an **electromagnet.** It can pull things made of iron. To see how it works, let's use it to make a gong.

Put the electromagnet inside the jar. Tie the iron screw or nut to the end of the pencil with the thread and lay the pencil across the top of the jar.

Fasten one end of the electromagnet wire onto one terminal of the dry cell. Then tap the other end against the other screw. Tap, take away, tap, take away. What happens? How is the sound made?

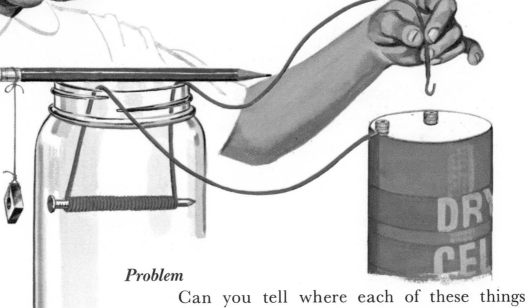

Problem

Can you tell where each of these things happens?

Electricity makes magnetism.

Magnetism moves iron.

Moving iron makes glass vibrate.

Vibrating glass makes air vibrate.

Vibrating air makes the eardrum vibrate.

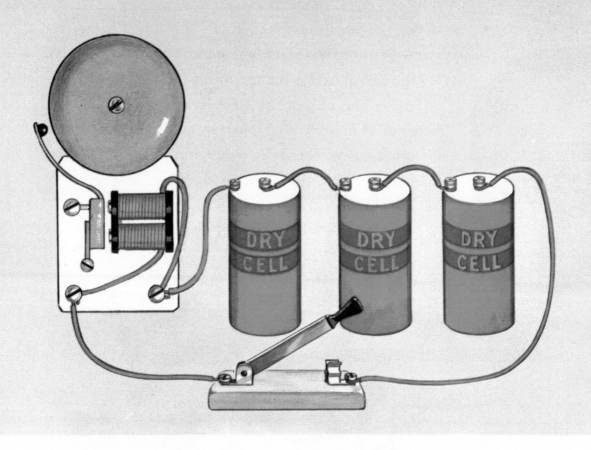

Electricity into Work

Here is a school gong. How many electromagnets does it have? Where is the part that strikes the gong? What makes this part move?

You have seen how electromagnets can make something move back and forth. They can also make something move around and around.

In some electric motors there are electromagnets that make an iron wheel spin around. The spinning iron wheel then turns the blades of a fan, or the hands of a clock, or some other machine.

Each one of these machines
has an electric motor inside.
Can you tell what each electric
motor does?

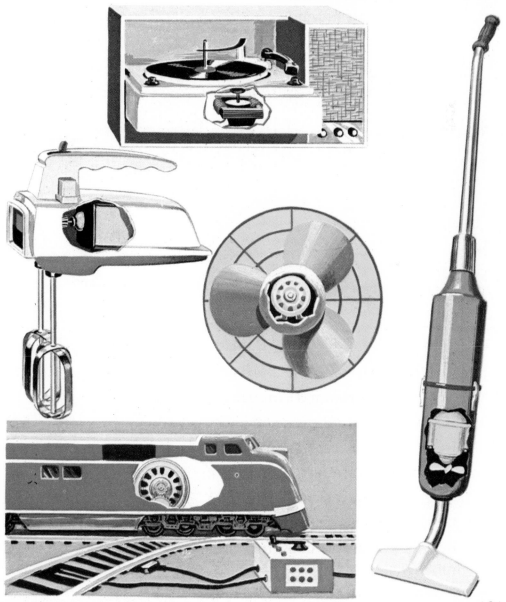

Electricity Stops and Goes

You have seen how electricity can make a filament glow and give off light. But the filament in a bulb is deep inside. How do we bring electricity to it? Let's follow the path of the electricity.

Electricity flows out of one terminal of the dry cell. It flows through one wire into the bulb. It flows through the filament. Then it flows through the second wire back to the other terminal.

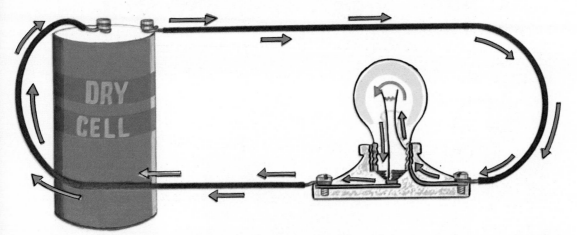

A complete path like this is called a **complete circuit.** Does the word *circuit* remind you of the word *circle?* How is a complete circuit like a circle?

When you have a complete circuit, the bulb lights up. Now how would you make the light go out? You could take away one of the wires. Then you would have an incomplete circuit.

But that's not the way you turn off the lights in your house. You always use a switch. Let's see how a switch works.

EXPERIMENT

You will need a dry cell,
three pieces of insulated
wire, a small lamp socket,
a flashlight bulb, a small
block of wood, two thumb-
tacks with metal heads, and
an aluminum food container
such as a pie tin.

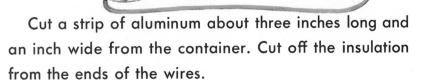

Cut a strip of aluminum about three inches long and
an inch wide from the container. Cut off the insulation
from the ends of the wires.

Push a thumbtack through the aluminum strip and
partway into the wood. Then push another thumbtack
partway into the wood, about two inches away.

Now join the wires as in the picture and push the
thumbtacks all the way in.

Push the strip of aluminum against the thumbtack.
Does the bulb light? Then lift it up. What happens now?
Move the strip down and up. Watch the light go on and
off.

You have made an electric switch.

Problem

Aluminum is a metal. The thumbtacks and
wires are made of metal, too. What else in the
circuit is made of metal?

Problem

Can you trace the metal path of a complete circuit? Can you then trace it in an incomplete circuit?

A real switch has a metal strip, too. When you push a handle or pull a chain, you move the strip into place. You make a complete circuit. The light goes on. How do you make an incomplete circuit?

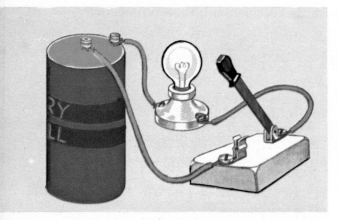 

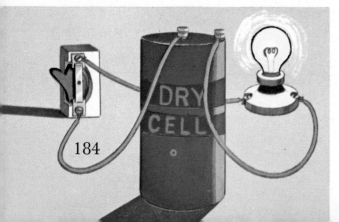 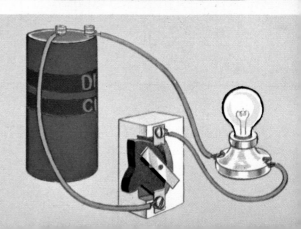

184

You can use the things you have learned about bulbs and switches in this way. You can help make a place in which to give plays.

OBSERVE AND FIND OUT

1. What things are run by electricity in your home? Make a chart like this and put the things under these headings.

HEAT FROM ELECTRICITY	LIGHT FROM ELECTRICITY	MOTION FROM ELECTRICITY

2. What different kinds of switches are in your home? What different kinds of switches are at school?

3. Look for several kinds of dry cells. Can you find out how each one is different? What is each one used for?

FIND OUT THROUGH EXPERIMENTS

1. Make an electromagnet like the one on page 178. Use it to pick up a paper clip. When you turn off the current, does the nail stop being a magnet right away, or does it take time? How can you find out?

2. Make three electromagnets. Make one with 10 turns of wire, one with 20 turns, and one with 30 turns. Pick up paper clips or tacks with each. Does the number of turns of wire change the way the electromagnet works? If so, in what way?

3. Make a bell ring. Use a dry cell, 3 wires, a switch and an electric bell. When the bell rings, see if you can find out how the electromagnets work in the bell.

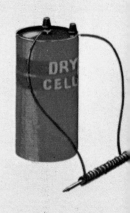

FIND OUT FROM OTHERS

1. Go to an electric supply store or to an electrician.
   a. Find out what kind of wire is used in light bulb filaments.

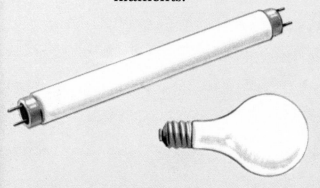

   b. Look at different kinds of light bulbs. Do they give off different amounts of light?
   c. Does the wire in a light bulb burn? If not, what does it do?
2. With a grown-up, explore the electrical wiring in your home.
   a. Where do wires from the powerhouse come into the house?
   b. Look for the electric meter, the main switch, and the fuse box.
   c. Find the cables that go from the fuse box into some room in the house.

FIND OUT FROM BOOKS

What is an electric insulator? Where are some materials that are used as electric insulators?

187

188

10

Moon, Planets, and Stars

Someday it may happen.

It may happen before you are grown up!

A rocket ship with people in it will be sent to the moon.

Let's pretend that everything is ready. The scientists are ready to aim the moon rocket. Should they aim it at the moon?

No! If they aim the rocket at the moon, it will never get there.

Scientists say they will aim it somewhere else. Where? And why? You can do an experiment to find out where to aim.

You will need a large ball, chalk, and a helper.

You will be the earth, your helper will be the moon, and the ball will be the rocket ship.

Draw a large circle on the ground. You (the earth) stand in the center of the circle. The moon person stands on the circle. The circle is the path of the moon as it moves around the earth. This path is called an **orbit**.

The moon starts to walk quickly along its orbit. Now you are ready to send your ball rocket to the moon! As the moon comes in front of you, roll the ball at him. Did you hit the moon?

You aimed the ball at the place where you saw the moon. But while the ball was rolling, the moon was moving. When the ball reached the orbit of the moon, the moon had already moved on to a new place in its orbit.

Problem

1. If you want the ball rocket to hit the moon, you should not aim it at the moon. Should you aim it in front of or behind the moon? Why?

2. How much ahead of the moon should you aim the ball rocket? You could try again and again until you got it right. You could use the same ball again and again.

But a real rocket cannot be used again and again. Also, a real rocket costs a lot of money. So the scientists must aim the rocket right the first time. To aim it right they must know many things. Three things are very important. Try to guess what these three things are before you read ahead. It will help you if you do the experiment again while you try to guess.

The three things are:

    1. How fast is the rocket going?

    2. How fast is the moon going?

    3. How far is the moon from the earth?

191

Here are the facts:

1. A rocket ship to the moon will travel about 25,000 miles an hour at top speed. After a while it will begin to slow down. Scientists say that as it gets closer to the moon it will speed up again.

2. The moon travels more than 2,000 miles an hour. At some parts of its orbit it goes faster than at other parts.

3. The moon is about 240,000 miles from the earth.

Now do you know where to aim the rocket? It would take a person many years to do all the arithmetic for one trip to the moon. But we don't have to. Scientists can feed all the facts into a machine. The machine can do all the arithmetic in a few minutes.

Rocket Engines

How will we go to the moon? And how will we get back? Airplanes cannot be used, because they need air to fly in. There is no air on the moon. There is no air most of the way between the earth and the moon. But we can go in rocket ships with rocket engines.

How does a rocket engine work? You can find out with a balloon.

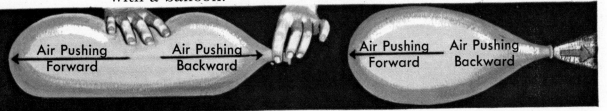

Air Pushing Forward   Air Pushing Backward   Air Pushing Forward   Air Pushing Backward

EXPERIMENT

Blow up a balloon and hold it at the neck. Push it at the front. Feel the air pushing back at you. Push the sides. Feel the air push back. Any place you push, the air pushes right back.

Now let go of the balloon. What happens?

When you let go, you let air go out. This air was pushing against the inside of the balloon before you let it go. Now it is just rushing out. But the air at the front of the balloon is still pushing forward. So the balloon goes forward.

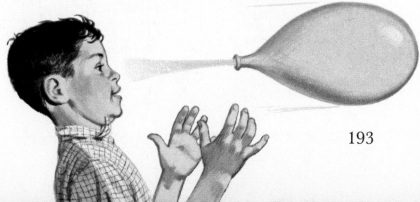

In a real rocket engine there is no air rushing out. Instead, there are very hot gases. These gases have much more push than the air in your balloon.

Rocket engines will send the first moon travelers on their way. Rocket engines will bring them back from the moon.

Here are some ways to use a balloon as a rocket engine. Study each picture. Can you use these pictures to explain how a real rocket engine works?

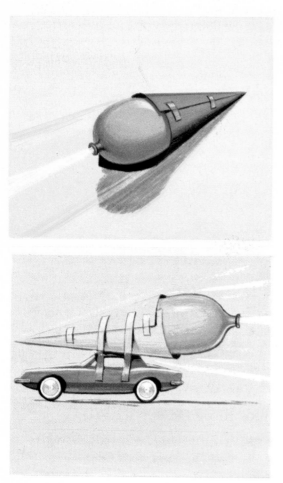

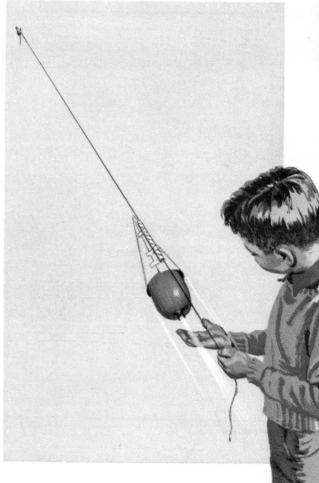

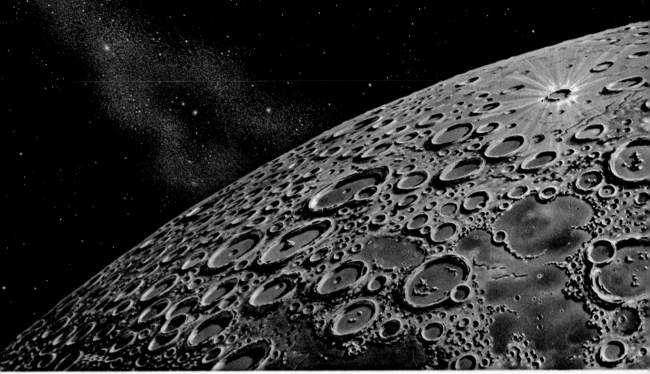

Almost There

When the moon travelers are almost there, what will they see? Will *everything* seem strange and new to them? No! Scientists have studied the moon for hundreds of years. At first they used small telescopes, then bigger ones. Now they can use photographs taken by cameras on rocket ships.

Look at the flat plains. Find some ring-shaped mountains. Some have peaks inside. Look for some round hollows called **craters.** The smallest crater in this picture is only about as large as a football field!

What made the rings and craters? Are there caves in the rocks? Are the rocks like those on earth? We have so many questions that can't be answered until we get there!

Ready for Moon Landing!

When we come close to the moon, we don't want to crash. We want to come down slowly and gently. Scientists say that rocket engines can help us land safely. Let's see how.

EXPERIMENT

You will need a balloon, some thread, two corks, and a piece of cardboard like this.

Tie one cork to the cardboard. Push the neck of the balloon through the middle hole.

Fill the balloon with air. Hold it up high while somebody holds the second cork next to it. Let both fall at the same time. What happens?

Read page 193 again. Then tell how the balloon in this experiment kept one cork from falling fast.

Balloons cannot be used for a real moon landing. Instead there will be small rocket engines shooting out hot gases. Which way should the gases come out? Which way will the gases push against the moon ship?

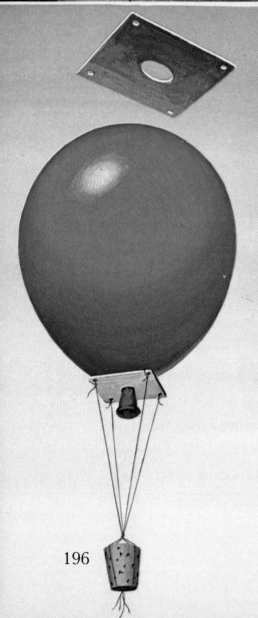

On the Moon

When the travelers land, what will they see? Scientists think the moon will look something like this. Rock mountains, rock and dust, not a drop of water, not one living thing—that is what scientists think the travelers will find.

The travelers must be careful not to touch anything with their bare hands. The sunlit rocks are hotter than boiling water. The shady places are much colder than a freezer. This is because the moon has no air. Air on the earth is like a thick, soft blanket. It keeps the sun from making the earth too hot. It keeps the shady places from becoming too cold.

Let's go back home, back to earth!

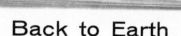

Back to Earth

How shall we make a safe landing on the earth? We can use rockets like the ones that landed us on the moon. But there is an easier way. We can use air to slow us down. We can do this with a parachute. Let's see how.

EXPERIMENT

You will need a handkerchief, some thread, and two corks.

Tie the corners of the handkerchief to one cork.

Hold the "parachute" up high. Hold the second cork next to it. Let them both fall. Which falls more slowly?

The "parachute" had to push air out of the way. This slowed the fall of the "parachute" and its cork. Did the other cork have to push as much air out of the way? Why not?

Problem

How should a parachute for heavy things be different from a parachute for light things? Why?

The Moon's Changing Shape

Sometimes the moon looks like a whole circle. Sometimes the moon looks like a half circle. At other times the moon looks like a slice of lemon peel.

Why does the shape of the moon change all the time? You can find out by doing this experiment.

EXPERIMENT

You will need an electric light, a ball, a few sheets of black paper, and a piece of white chalk.

In this experiment the ball will be the moon. The electric light will be the sun. You will be the earth.

In this experiment you will make the moon travel around you. The real moon travels, too. It travels around the real earth.

You will use the electric light to shine on the little moon. The real moon has light shining on it, too. The light comes from the sun.

Darken the room. Sit with the light to your left, as in the picture.

Hold the ball in front of you, a little higher than your head. See the sun shining on the moon. How much of the moon is really lit up? Can you see all the lit-up side?

Make a picture of what you see. Use white chalk on black paper. Check to see if your picture looks like any of the moon shapes in the pictures on page 201. If so, which one?

Now make your moon travel like the real one. Move the ball slowly to the left until you reach place 2. Make a picture of what you see. Does it look like any of the pictures on page 201? If so, which one?

How much of the moon is really lit up? Can you see all of the lit-up side?

Keep the moon traveling to the left. Stop at each number. Make a picture of what you see. Find a picture like it at the bottom of this page.

How much of the moon is always lit up?

Why don't we always see all the lit-up side?

Now you know about the changing shape of the moon. It seems to change as the moon travels around the earth. As it travels, we see less and less of the lit-up side. Then we see more and more.

Over and over again, we see these changes of the moon. They are called the moon's **phases.** The moon goes through all its phases in about four weeks.

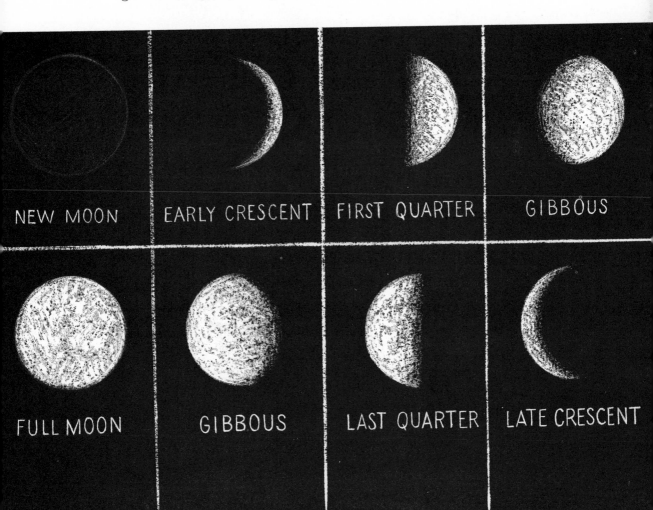

NEW MOON   EARLY CRESCENT   FIRST QUARTER   GIBBOUS

FULL MOON   GIBBOUS   LAST QUARTER   LATE CRESCENT

Pluto

Neptune

Saturn

Uranus

Jupiter

Off to the Planets

After the first few trips to the moon, scientists may plan trips to the planets. We are already on one of the planets. The other planets are like the earth in some ways. They are large and round. They travel around the sun in orbits. They get light and heat from the sun.

There are nine planets in our solar system. The nearest to the sun is Mercury. Then come Venus, Earth, Mars, Jupiter, Saturn, Uranus, Neptune, and Pluto. Find them in the pictures.

Which one would you choose for the first trip to a planet? You would probably choose the planet most like the earth. Is there a planet with water, oxygen in the air, and comfortable temperatures?

Or are some planets like the moon? Remember, the moon has no air and no water. It is dry, rocky, and dusty. Its temperatures are both too high and too low. You would freeze in the shade and broil in the sunlight.

Let's find out some of the important facts about each planet.

This chart will help you to choose a planet for the first trip. Scientists have worked out the travel times shown below.

Planet	Oxygen	Water	Temperature degrees F.		Are Living Things Present	Travel Time To The Planets
			Day	Night		
Mercury	none	none	750	−450	none	150 days
Venus	traces	traces	800	800	none at surface	110 days
Earth	yes	yes	70	60	yes	--------
Mars	traces	traces	50	−94	?	260 days
Jupiter	none	none	−220	?	no	2 years
Saturn	none	none	−238	?	no	6 years
Uranus	none	none	−300	?	no	16 years
Neptune	none	none	−346	?	no	31 years
Pluto	none	none	−348	?	no	46 years

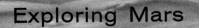

Exploring Mars

Did you find that Mars is the planet most like the earth? Its warmest daytime temperature is comfortable enough. The nighttime temperature is quite cold, but some places on the earth are even colder. Do you think you will have to take along oxygen?

Stretches of land that change from green to brown have been seen through telescopes. Explorers will be able to tell whether they are plants that change with the seasons. Most scientists think there are no animals.

White caps have been seen on the north and south poles of Mars. These caps slowly shrink and disappear during the summer season at each pole. Scientists think they are layers of frost or thin snow. If so, they may be a water supply for the explorers.

So a trip to Mars doesn't seem too impossible, someday. What about a trip to any of the other planets? Just look at that chart again!

205

A Trip to the Stars?

Scientists do not think that we will ever get to the stars.

Stars are huge, hot suns. Many of them are larger and hotter than our sun. The nearest star is millions of times farther away than our sun.

Like our sun, the stars shine brightly all the time, night and day.

Night and day? Then why don't we see any stars in the daytime? Here is a way to find out.

EXPERIMENT

Make some pinholes in a piece of wax paper and in a piece of black paper. Fasten both to a windowpane. In which paper can you see the pinholes more clearly? Why?

How does this explain why the stars seem to disappear at sunrise and appear again after sunset?

When the moon is out in the daytime, it does not seem as bright as it does at night. Can you explain why? You could cut two shapes, as shown in the picture below, to help you with your explanation.

Constellations

Some stars seem to be in groups whose shape we can see easily. These groups are called constellations.

Four constellations are easy to find. Face north. Then hold your arm like this. Look for the North Star, almost in line with your finger.

This picture shows the four constellations as you would see them about 9 o'clock on a January night. What month is it now? Turn the book so that the present month is at the top of the circle. You will see how the constellations look at 9 o'clock tonight. Will you see lines between the stars?

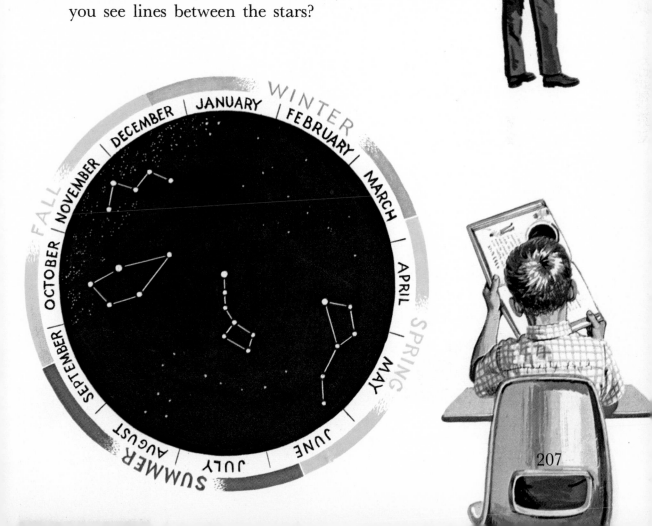

207

OBSERVE AND FIND OUT

1. Are stars always in the same place?
   a. Early, on a clear evening, go outdoors. Choose a bright star. Move around until the star is just above a chimney or a tree. Mark the spot where you stand.
   b. Go outdoors an hour later. Stand in the marked spot. Look at the chimney or tree. Is the star still over it? If not, in which direction has it moved?
   c. There is one star called Polaris (the North Star) that will always seem to be in the same spot. It doesn't seem to move. Can you find that star?
2. Find out about moon travel. Plan to go outdoors at the same time on two clear nights in a row. You might even be lucky and see the moon twice in a row during the daytime.
   a. Find the moon. Move yourself to a place where the moon is just above a tree or chimney. Mark your spot and write down the time. Make a picture of the moon and the chimney.
   b. On the next night go back to the same spot at the same time. Is the moon in the same place? Make a drawing of where you see it.

208

FIND OUT FROM NUMBERS

1. This picture shows the size of the earth compared to the size of the moon.

    a. Measure across each circle. How many times does the moon circle fit on the earth circle?

    b. The real moon is about 2000 miles across. Can you tell about how wide the earth is?

2. This is a way to get an idea of the moon's distance from the earth. Use a grapefruit for the earth and a ping-pong ball for the moon. (A large grapefruit is about four times as wide as a ping-pong ball.)

    a. Measure the grapefruit as it is done in the picture. Put the grapefruit on the floor at one end of the room.

    b. Cut a piece of thread that is as long as 30 grapefruits. Stretch it from the grapefruit across the room.

    c. Put the ping-pong ball on the floor at the end of the string.

    d. Which of these pictures shows what you found out?

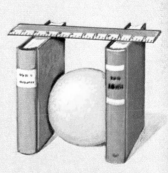

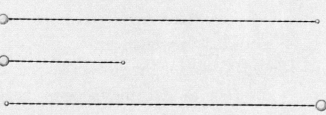

210

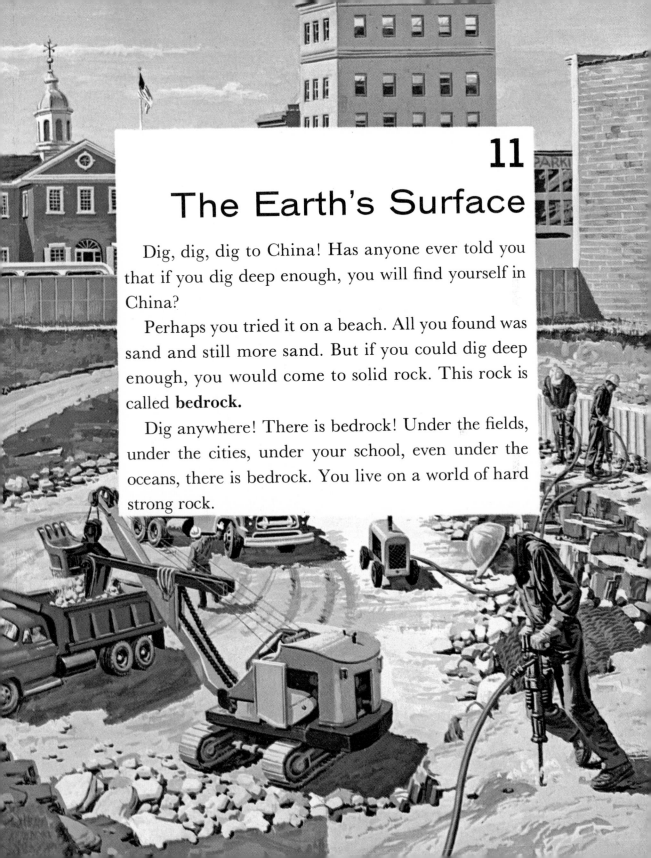

The Earth's Surface

Dig, dig, dig to China! Has anyone ever told you that if you dig deep enough, you will find yourself in China?

Perhaps you tried it on a beach. All you found was sand and still more sand. But if you could dig deep enough, you would come to solid rock. This rock is called **bedrock.**

Dig anywhere! There is bedrock! Under the fields, under the cities, under your school, even under the oceans, there is bedrock. You live on a world of hard strong rock.

Does the earth's surface where you live look rocky? Does it look like any of the places in the picture? The earth's surface does not look the same everywhere. Only some places are rocky. Some are covered with soil.

In this soil grow most of the green plants of the world. Green plants make the food that living things need. Most plants grow in soil.

Most soil has rock in it. You can learn about rocks in soil by doing the next experiment.

EXPERIMENT

You will need a quart jar, some garden soil, a bowl, a magnifying lens, and water.

Put some soil into a jar of water. Shake it up. Then let it stand for a while.

Slowly pour off the water into a bowl. Observe the water in the bowl. Does it look the same as when you poured it into the jar? If there are any bits of soil in it, feel them. Are they hard or soft? Look at them under a magnifying lens. What do you think some of them are? Give your reasons.

Now take some soil from the bottom of the jar. Rub it between your fingers. Do you feel rough bits in it? Does it feel like sand?

Look at some of this soil under a magnifying lens. Are the pieces all the same size? Are they the same shape? Are they the same color? What do you think these pieces are? Give your reasons.

213

A Rocky Surface

The earth has many rocky places. There are high mountains of rock with tops covered by snow and ice. There are rocky places that go right down to the sea.

All these huge mountains of hard rock are being broken into tiny bits.

What hammers are strong enough to break huge mountains into tiny bits?

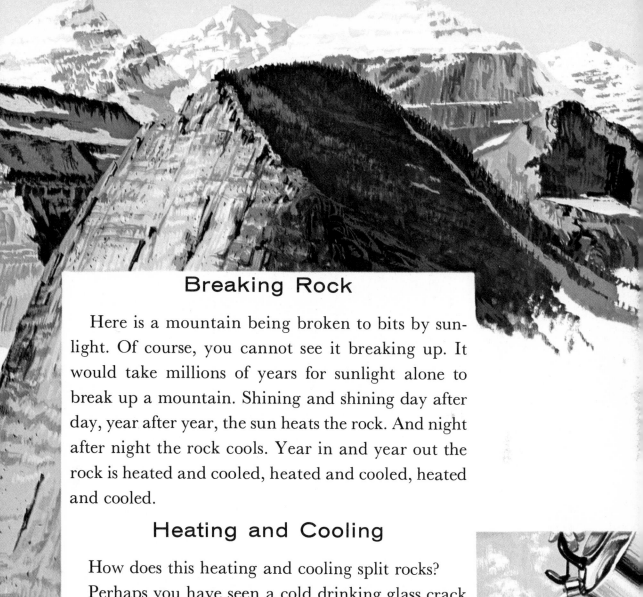

Breaking Rock

Here is a mountain being broken to bits by sunlight. Of course, you cannot see it breaking up. It would take millions of years for sunlight alone to break up a mountain. Shining and shining day after day, year after year, the sun heats the rock. And night after night the rock cools. Year in and year out the rock is heated and cooled, heated and cooled, heated and cooled.

Heating and Cooling

How does this heating and cooling split rocks?

Perhaps you have seen a cold drinking glass crack when very hot water is poured into it.

A hot glass can break when cold water is poured into it.

How does a change in temperature make some things crack? Look at the picture on the right. Here is a way to help you find out.

215

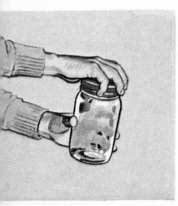

TRY THIS

You will need a clean, empty jar with a screw cover and some hot water.

Screw the cover on so tightly that it is too hard for you to open. Then run hot water over the cover only.

Dry it. Now try to open it. Is it easier now?

Why did the cover come off easily?

The heat of the hot water made the cover bigger. Most things become bigger when they are heated. We say they **expand.**

When things expand, they take up more space. When things are cooled, they become smaller. We say they **contract.**

When hot water is poured into a cold drinking glass, the inside of the glass gets hot and expands more quickly than the outside. This makes a crack in the glass.

The same thing happens on the mountain. Which part of the rock expands more quickly in the sunlight —the outside or the inside? When does the rock contract?

Day and night the mountain is heated and cooled. The surface rock expands and contracts. At last a piece splits away. The earth's gravity pulls it down.

16

Problem

Some things are built to expand and contract without breaking. Concrete sidewalks have cracks built into them. On a hot day concrete sidewalks have space to expand without breaking. Are the spaces the biggest when the temperature is high or when it is low? Why?

Train tracks, too, are laid with a little space between the pieces of track. In the hot sunlight the tracks get a little bigger. The tracks can expand without breaking. When is the space the smallest?

217

Water and Rock

Mountains never seem to change, but they really do. A great changer is water. Moving water can cut down the highest, hardest mountain.

Every little stream, every brook, every river works like a saw cutting away at the rock underneath.

Gravity keeps pulling the water down, always down. The water carries along grains of sand and bits of pebbles and stones that scratch and cut at the rock.

218

In a fast-rushing river big rocks are rolled along. They bang and smash as they go. Pebbles click and clatter against each other and against the rock of the riverbed. The sand is rushed along, scratching and rubbing as it goes.

A bit at a time, a grain here and a pebble there, the flowing water cuts deeper and deeper into its rocky bed.

Over millions of years the rock mountain is cut apart. Stones, pebbles, and fine sand are carried down by flowing water, pulled by gravity. Can you guess what happens to all these pieces of rock?

As it reaches flatter land, the river slows down. It may wander through farmlands and curve gently in and out of fields.

Flowing water carries along many things. It carries broken rock, mud, sand, soil, bits of old leaves, and twigs. All these different things in the water are called **sediment.**

What happens to sediment in water that flows quickly? What happens to sediment when water slows down? You can find out in the following experiment.

EXPERIMENT

You will need some garden soil, a jar, a measuring cup, and water.

Mix one cup of soil with two cups of water in a jar. Shake it. What is happening to the sediment when you are shaking the jar? Let it stand for a while. What do you observe?

Problem

Find a picture of a river that is like the jar when it is shaken. Find a picture of a river that is like the jar when it has been standing.

What is being carried in the fast-moving part of the river? What are some things that the slow river is dropping? What do you think the river bottom is like in the picture on page 220? On page 219? Tell why you think so.

Ice Breaks Rock

Water breaks rock in other ways, too. You can see how for yourself.

FIND OUT

Fill an empty ice tray with water. Fill it to the top.

Let the water freeze. Now look at it. The ice is heaped higher than the top of the tray. When water changes to ice, it expands. It takes up more room.

As water freezes and expands, it can push very hard. In this experiment you will see how hard it can push.

EXPERIMENT

You will need two glass jars with covers, two paper bags, and water.

Fill one jar with water right to the top. Leave the other jar empty. Cover both jars tightly. Put both jars in paper bags. Close the tops of the bags.

Put them in a cold place. Let the water freeze.

What happened to the jar with water? Can you tell why? Why was the empty jar also used in this experiment?

Freezing water can break glass. It can also break rocks. When water flows into a crack in a rock and then freezes to ice, it expands. As it changes to ice, it pushes against the sides of the crack and splits the rock apart.

Year after year, a little at a time, rock mountains are broken apart by freezing water. In this picture what did freezing water do? What did gravity do?

Plants Break Rock

These plants can grow on rock. As they grow, they soften the rock until it crumbles a little. If you pick off a piece of the plant, you can see bits of soft, crumbly rock underneath.

As the rock is crumbled, other plants can grow on it. Plants die. They crumble into the soil, along with bits of crumbled rock.

Soil

There are many kinds of plants and many kinds of rocks. Do you think there are many kinds of soils, too? Here is how you can find out for yourself.

EXPERIMENT

Bring in soil from different places. Try to get soil from each of these: a farm, a woods, the bank of a brook or river, a place where a house or road is being built.

Put a cupful of each kind of soil into jars. Add water until each jar is almost full. Put the covers on tightly and shake the jars. Let the jars stand until the water is almost clear.

Do any of the jars have different layers of soil? Which layer has the largest pieces? Is anything floating in the water? Feel it with your fingers. Can you tell that this is plant material? Does each jar have the same amount of plant material?

Use a spoon to get some of the other layers of sediment. Feel the sediment with your fingers. Does it feel like sand or pebbles? What kind of sediment does each jar have the most of?

All of these soils are part of the earth's surface. You know how rocks are turned to soil. Rocks are broken and crumbled by plants, running water, and ice. The earth's surface is always changing.

226

Rushing rivers, slow rivers, and rivers of ice write their story across the earth's surface.

A river may make a deep cut through high mountains, forming a canyon. Can you find one here?

Over millions of years, water and gravity may wear down a steep canyon and make a gentle valley.

Sometimes the river carries its sediment all the way to the end of the river and drops it there. Here it may build new land called a **delta.**

Look at the pictures on these pages. How may water and gravity have helped to make each place?

DISCUSS AND FIND OUT

1. Why is good soil so important to us?

2. Is the entire earth made of rock? What is found beneath the oceans and rivers? What is soil made of? Do mountains change? If so, what makes them change?

DO THIS AND FIND OUT

1. Spread half a teaspoon of sand on graph paper with small squares.

   a. Are the little grains of sand all the same size?
   b. Are the grains all the same shape?
   c. Use a magnifying glass and see whether they might have come from the same rock or from different rocks.
   d. First guess and then count the number of grains on one square.

2. Get a piece of wire screen. Put some soil on it. Shake the screen back and forth over a piece of white paper. See if any small pieces of rock are left on the screen. How much of the soil goes through the screen?

EXPLORE AND FIND OUT

1. Take a trip to look for large rocks with cracks in them. Are there any plants growing in the cracks? Can you find a cracked rock that has a tree growing in it?

2. Go to a place where the soil has been dug out and there is a good steep bank.

    a. Are there plants at the top of the bank? How far into the soil have the roots grown?

    b. What color is the soil at the top of the bank?

    c. Are there different layers of soil?

    d. What color is the soil at the bottom of the bank?

    e. Are there rocks along the bank? Are they large or small?

EXPERIMENT AND FIND OUT

What happens to bare soil in the rain? To find out, spread some soil on a board like this. Put a pan at the lower end. Sprinkle water on the soil at the upper end. What kind of soil washes down the board? Is the soil in the pan pebbly or very fine?

FIND OUT FROM BOOKS

1. What are some plants that grow on rocks? Find out what is different about the roots of these plants.

2. Look up ways that plants and animals help to make soil better for growing plants.

229

12
Learning About Rocks

These geologists are reading a story in a rock. It is a long, long story. A **geologist** is a scientist who studies the earth and its rocks. He can tell how these colored layers of rocks were made.

Looking at these old Indian houses, the geologist can tell what kinds of rocks were used. He can even tell that the rocks were cut by other rocks. How can rocks be cut with rocks?

231

Long ago the Indians who lived here found such a way. They found that some rocks are much harder than others. They made tools out of hard rocks. With these tools they broke the softer rocks. They broke them into blocks.

It was hard work, but they worked together and built big, cool houses. They made homes of soft rocks that they cut with tools of hard rocks.

The best way to learn about rocks is by studying the rocks themselves. Rocks are different in softness and hardness. Can you think of some other differences?

232

FIND OUT

Bring in a few small rocks. Let each one in your class try to find them in different places.

Spread the rocks on newspaper and look at them. Are they all the same color? Do they seem to be made of the same materials? Feel them. Are they smooth or rough? Pick up two of about the same size, one in each hand. Do they weigh about the same?

Put some in water. Do the same things happen to each? Take them out. Do some dry faster than others? Do some have layers? If you tap them gently, do some break? You can tell by looking and touching.

A geologist learns about rocks by observing and testing them. You can learn by doing some of these tests yourself.

Testing Rock

Any rock feels hard when you stub your toe on it. How can you tell how hard a rock is? Here is one way to test the hardness of rocks.

You will need different kinds of rocks.

Bring some rocks to school. Select any two of them and try to scratch one rock with the other. The one that makes a scratch mark is harder. The softer rock will not scratch the harder rock.

Try scratching other pairs of rocks. Which one of each pair leaves a scratch on the other?

Geologists test rocks for hardness. They use numbers to show how hard the rocks are. The numbers are called a hardness scale. The softest rocks have a hardness of 1. You can scratch them with your fingernail. The hardest rock material in the world is the diamond. It has a hardness of 10.

After you have tried scratching all your rocks, put them in order according to their hardness. Look at the hardness scale on page 235. What is the hardness number of your softest rock? Your hardest rock?

234

Hardness Scale

1   TALC   Scratch talc with No. 2 (gypsum).

2   GYPSUM   Scratch gypsum with your fingernail (or No. 3).

3   CALCITE   Scratch calcite with a penny (or No. 4).

4   FLUORITE   Scratch fluorite with No. 5 (apatite).

5   APATITE   Scratch apatite with a knife (or No. 6).

6   FELDSPAR   Scratch feldspar with a steel file (or No. 7).

7   QUARTZ   Scratch quartz with No. 8 (topaz).

8   TOPAZ   Scratch topaz with No. 9 (corundum).

9   CORUNDUM   Scratch corundum with No. 10 (diamond).

235

10   DIAMOND   No rock will scratch diamond.

Sandstone

Look at your rocks. Do some of them seem to be made of grains of sand stuck together? Do grains of sand rub off?

Some rocks really are made of grains of sand stuck together. These rocks are called **sandstone.**

Millions of years ago there was a huge sea that covered a large part of this country. Rivers flowed into this sea, bringing in sand and other sediment that sank slowly to the bottom.

More and more sediment flowed in and sank down. It heaped up higher and higher, heavier and heavier. The heavy heap squeezed down on the sediment below. The sediment became rock. Such rock is called **sedimentary rock.**

Ohio Sandstone

Coarse-grained Sandstone

Yellow Sandstone

Fine-grained Sandstone

Arkose

Red Sandstone

Gray Sandstone

In the seawater there were substances that stuck the sand grains together and made them into sandstone.

It took millions of years for loose sand at the bottom of the sea to be changed to sandstone. Still later the sea dried up and left the sandstone. Thick layers of it covered a large part of this country.

Indians used sandstone for building their homes in the desert. People still use it today. You may have seen city houses with front steps and walls made of sandstone.

What a long way that sandstone has traveled! Perhaps it was once part of a mountain. Before that it was at the bottom of the sea. Now it is part of a city house.

Clay

All clay is made from certain kinds of rocks. The rocks were broken into clay grains by sunlight, water, and plants. These grains are smaller than most sand grains. The small grains were carried away by water. They were piled up in heaps called **clay beds.**

Clay is a sedimentary material. It comes from rocks of different colors, so we find clay of different colors, too.

Clay is used for many things. Most dishes are made of clay. Plants grow in clay pots. Perhaps your school is built of clay bricks.

These people are building a house of one kind of clay brick. It is called **adobe brick.** Adobe brick is used only in dry places. You can make an adobe brick and find out why.

TRY THIS

You will need a milk carton, some clay, straw, and water.

Mix clay with cut-up straw and water. Pour this material into a milk carton you have cut down.

Leave the carton in the sun for a day or two.

Then take out your brick and finish drying it.

239

You know that when clay is mixed with water it becomes soft. It can be made into many shapes. When the wet clay is dried, it becomes hard. What happens when this kind of clay gets wet again? Plan an experiment with these materials to show what happens.

EXPERIMENT

You will need either your adobe brick or a lump of dry clay, a bowl of water, and a stirring spoon.

Put the brick or clay in the bowl of water. Leave it there for a while and then stir it.

What happens to the clay? What happens to the water? Why do you think this happens?

Can you tell why adobe is used only in dry places?

Do all things made of clay crumble in water?

Do the next experiment to find out.

EXPERIMENT

You will need a piece of a broken clay flowerpot, some pieces of broken clay dishes, a bowl, and water.

Put the pieces in a bowl of water. Leave them there for a while and then stir the water. Does the water become cloudy?

Do the pieces of clay become soft and crumbly?

Heat Changes Clay

Perhaps you have made things of soft clay, as in the picture below.

Clay can be baked in hot ovens called **kilns.** The clay things are put into the kiln. Then the heat is turned on for a while. The heat comes from an electric heater or from a gas flame. The clay things are baked and become harder and stronger.

Heat changes clay.

Clay Dishes

Bring in some pieces of broken china, flowerpots, and other clay things. Look at the broken edges. You will see there are many kinds and colors of clay.

When the grains of clay are very small, we can make very smooth, thin dishes.

Clay with larger grains is used for flowerpots, bricks, and other things that do not have to be smooth.

Clay beds are found in many parts of the world. They are found even in dry, desert places. If you found a clay bed in a desert, what would you know about the history of the place?

Today people dig up different kinds of clay to make bricks, dishes, and many other useful things. Perhaps you ate breakfast on a plate that was part of a mountain millions of years ago.

All Kinds of Sedimentary Rock

Look back at the experiment on page 221. The first sediments to drop to the bottom were the gravel and pebbles. Now look at the picture at the bottom of this page.

When a river flows into the ocean, the first sediments to drop to the bottom are the heavy gravel and pebbles.

The lighter sediments may be carried a little farther out in the water. Usually the sand settles next. After that the clays settle to the bottom.

Conglomerate

Sandstones

Clay

Shale

Different kinds of sediment form different kinds of sedimentary rocks.

Pebbles that stick together form a rock called **pudding stone.** Can you tell why?

You know there are many kinds of sandstone made of different kinds of sand.

When clay is squeezed down hard, it forms a rock called **shale.** There are many kinds of shales, made of different kinds of clay. The picture on page 243 shows one kind of shale.

Pudding stone, sandstone, and shale are all sedimentary rocks. But they are not the only sedimentary rock. Another kind is shown below.

Limestone

Some sedimentary rock is formed in another way. Many animals with shells live in the ocean. When they die, their shells drop to the bottom of the ocean, just as other sediments do.

Layer upon layer is built up. After millions of years, the loose shells at the bottom of the ocean are changed to sedimentary rock. Rock formed in this way is called **limestone.**

244

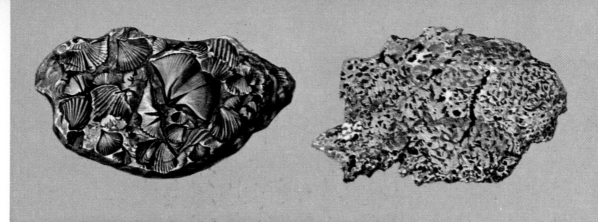

In some limestone you can still see bits of shell. Other kinds of limestone are rough and hard and you cannot see any shells in them.

Geologists have a test for limestone which you can do in your classroom.

EXPERIMENT

You will need different kinds of rocks and some vinegar or lemon juice.

Scratch some rocks with harder rocks as you did on page 234. Pour a few drops of vinegar or lemon juice on the scratches.

Do any of them bubble like soda water? All limestone bubbles when tested this way. Now you know two tests that geologists use on rocks.

Different layers of sand, different layers of clay,
different layers of pebbles and shells—all make different layers of sedimentary rock.

Sediments may change. The river that brings the
sediments to the ocean may be wearing away new
kinds of rock. The river may carry more sediments
when there is a flood. It may carry different kinds of
pebbles, or sand, or clay.

Problem

What will happen if a layer of red clay is
dropped on top of a layer of white clay? If a layer
of sand is dropped on top of a layer of shale?

Fossils

When you hunt for rocks, you may be lucky and find one with a fish shape in it. Or maybe one like this.

Millions of years ago animals that lived in the water died and fell into the sediments. The hard parts of the animals, such as bones and shells, remained in these sediments when they became rock.

Sometimes an animal left its footprint in wet mud. When the mud dried and hardened to stone, the footprint could still be seen.

These remains of living things left in the rock are called **fossils.**

Fossils help us find out about plants and animals that lived millions of years ago.

This huge dinosaur lived 30 million years ago! At one time there were many kinds of dinosaurs, but they have all died out.

247

TRY THIS AND FIND OUT

1. Collect some interesting rocks. Spread out the rocks on a newspaper. Follow the directions on page 234. Answer each of the questions carefully and learn about your own collection.

2. Next read page 235 again. Figure out where each rock in your collection belongs on the hardness scale. Make a hardness scale in your notebook. Write in the names of some of your rocks.

3. Collect a handful of sand, a handful of dry mud, and a handful of clay. Mix each with water. Squeeze out the water. What happens? Leave each squeezed sample on a paper in the sun. Let it dry. What changes do you see? Do all the samples change the same way?

	Hardness scale	Rock samples
1.	Talc	
2.	Gypsum	
3.	Calcite	

FIND OUT THROUGH AN EXPERIMENT

Half-fill a glass jar with sandy and pebbly soil. Add water nearly to the top of the jar. Screw the cap on tight. Shake the jar. Let it stand. Watch what happens. Where are the big grains? Where are the tiniest grains? Are there layers in the jar? How could this become a rock?

EXPLORE AND FIND OUT

Take a field trip to a place where a road has been cut through rocks. Look at the rocks carefully. Are there layers? What colors are they? How hard are they? Are they like rocks you have collected? Can you find pictures of rocks like these in a book on rocks?

FIND OUT FROM BOOKS

1. Which two rocks were most used by the Indians for making arrowheads?

2. Some sandstones are light-colored, some are dark, and others are red. Find out how this happens.

250

13

The Water Cycle

Have you ever been out in a pouring rain? Did you get soaked? Everything did—the houses, the trees, the ground. What a lot of water! Where did it all come from?

Then the rain stopped. Soon everything was dry again. Where did all that water go?

You know where some of the water goes. It flows into brooks. The brooks join and become rivers. In brooks and rivers the rainwater flows down and down. It flows down to the sea.

What about the rest of the rainwater? Where does it go? Does it ever come back? Can we catch it and use it?

Let's follow the travels of rainwater.

Underground Water

Some water soaks into the ground. When the ground is soaked, the water begins to flow away downhill. It flows underground through soil and rocks, until it reaches bedrock. Some of it may flow along the bedrock until it reaches an open place.

Perhaps you have felt a cool spot in a pond where underground water was flowing in. Perhaps you have seen underground water bubbling out in a spring where bedrock is near the surface.

Some of the water keeps flowing underground until it reaches the sea.

252

Evaporation

Some rainwater doesn't flow down. It stops for a while where it fell. Then it's gone. Where do you think the water goes? Let's see.

EXPERIMENT

Put three inches of water in each of two glasses. Put both glasses in a sunny, warm place. Cover one glass. Measure the water in each glass every day. How does the covered glass help you find the answer to the question above? Keep a record like this.

When water goes into the air, we say it evaporates. You cannot see it, because water evaporates in very tiny bits. It becomes water vapor. Find the word *vapor* in *evaporate*.

The water vapor spreads out into the air. If it becomes cool, it may form fog along the ground. The water vapor may be carried high up. Then, if it cools, it becomes a cloud. Both fog and clouds are made of tiny drops of water.

If the tiny drops are cooled still more, they stick to dust in the air. More and more tiny drops stick together. They form bigger drops, raindrops. Down comes the rain!

From earth to air and back to where it started—this is called a **cycle.** The travel of water is called a **water cycle.**

Over and over, up and down, the water cycle keeps going. This morning you washed your hands in water that is millions of years old.

Perhaps it was in a snowball that a boy threw ten thousand years ago. Perhaps it was in a puddle that you splashed in last week.

The water has traveled up to the clouds and down to the earth millions of times. Each time the sun warmed the water. It became clean water vapor. Then it became fog or clouds.

Each time it was cooled and fell, clean and fresh, upon the earth.

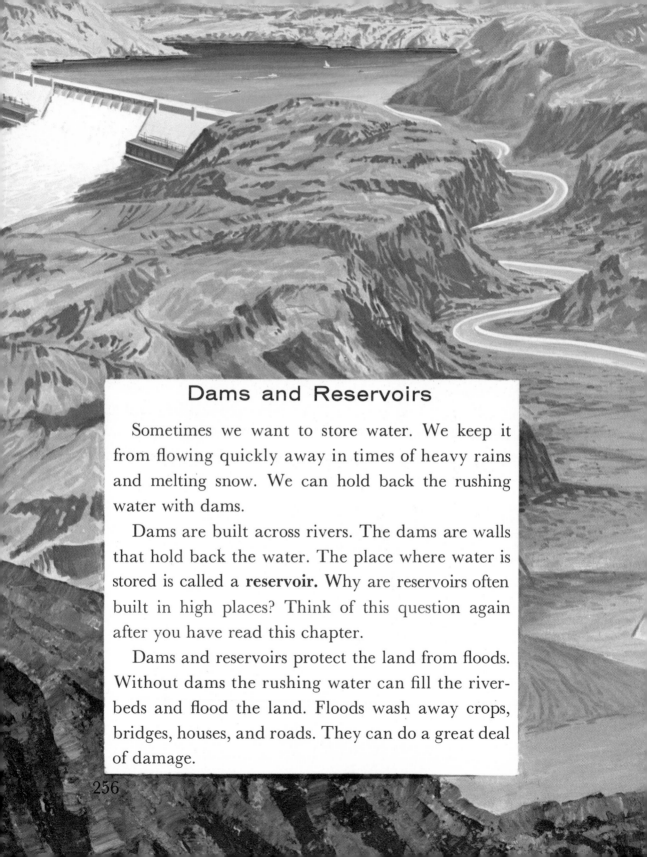

Dams and Reservoirs

Sometimes we want to store water. We keep it from flowing quickly away in times of heavy rains and melting snow. We can hold back the rushing water with dams.

Dams are built across rivers. The dams are walls that hold back the water. The place where water is stored is called a **reservoir.** Why are reservoirs often built in high places? Think of this question again after you have read this chapter.

Dams and reservoirs protect the land from floods. Without dams the rushing water can fill the river-beds and flood the land. Floods wash away crops, bridges, houses, and roads. They can do a great deal of damage.

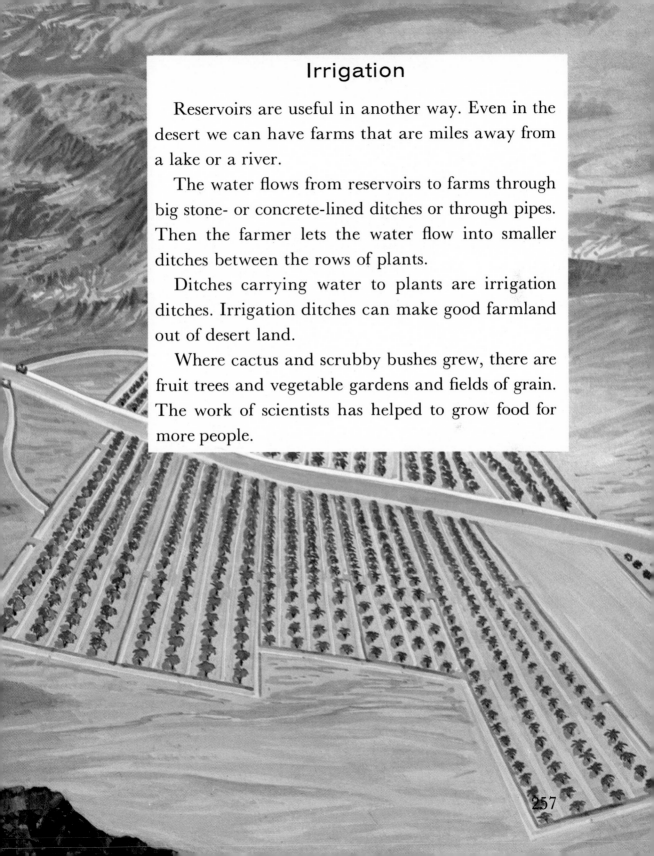

Irrigation

Reservoirs are useful in another way. Even in the desert we can have farms that are miles away from a lake or a river.

The water flows from reservoirs to farms through big stone- or concrete-lined ditches or through pipes. Then the farmer lets the water flow into smaller ditches between the rows of plants.

Ditches carrying water to plants are irrigation ditches. Irrigation ditches can make good farmland out of desert land.

Where cactus and scrubby bushes grew, there are fruit trees and vegetable gardens and fields of grain. The work of scientists has helped to grow food for more people.

Water Supply

We store water for another use. This high reservoir is full of cool, clean water. A few miles away there is a city where the people need the water for drinking. Should we use open ditches to bring the water from the reservoir to the city?

No, we should not! Dirt may fall in and make the water unfit for drinking. Drinking water must be very clean. We need something better than open ditches for bringing drinking water to the city.

We cannot use ditches for another reason. There are hills between the reservoir and the city.

258

Water and Gravity

Water can flow downhill easily. Can it flow uphill, too? You can find out for yourself.

TRY THIS

You will need a piece of foil and some water.

Fold a strip of foil into this shape. Pour water at the top. What makes the water go down? Does it go up the other side?

Water flows down because the earth's gravity pulls it. Gravity always pulls down toward the earth. It pulls things from higher to lower places.

Problem

Here is a map of a river flowing into a lake. Where is the higher land—near the house or near the trees?

Making Water Flow Up

How can we get the cool, clean water from the reservoir to the city? We could dig a tunnel through the hills, but that would be a lot of work and cost a lot of money. How can we get the water over the hill? Can we use the pull of gravity? Let's see.

EXPERIMENT

You will need a funnel, a rubber tube, and water.

Join a rubber tube to a funnel.

Hold the tube in the shape of a hill. Be sure that the funnel is a little higher than the hill, as shown in the picture. Then pour some water into the funnel. Does the water flow out of the tube?

In which part of the tube does water flow uphill? Can you tell how gravity does it?

It is easier to understand if you think of the tube in three parts.

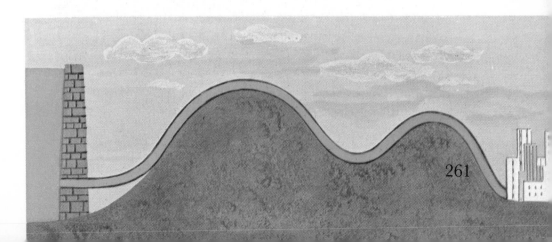

In part 1, which way does gravity pull the water? In part 2, which way does gravity pull the water? Part 1 is higher and has more water in it. Can it push against the water in part 2 and make it go up? What makes the water in part 3 flow down?

So the downward pull of gravity can make water flow up! We can build a pipe from the reservoir over the hill to the city. Of course, the reservoir must be higher than the city. Why?

Problem

Suppose there are two hills between the reservoir and the city. Can gravity make the water flow up twice? Plan an experiment to find out. Tell about gravity in each part of the pipe.

261

Water in the City

When the water gets to the city, it must flow up through pipes under the streets.

The pipes are called **water mains.** There are water mains under every street in the city. Each home and school, each store and factory, has pipes that reach up from the water mains.

Winter and summer, night and day, there is water for drinking and cooking and washing and playing. Water flows up into your bathtub, up into the kitchen sink, up into the park fountain. Water goes up from the water mains under the street.

262

Problem

In some cities the water does not come from a high place. Then it cannot flow up by itself. We must force it up by a pump.

Which way is used in your city, or in a city near you? Find out.

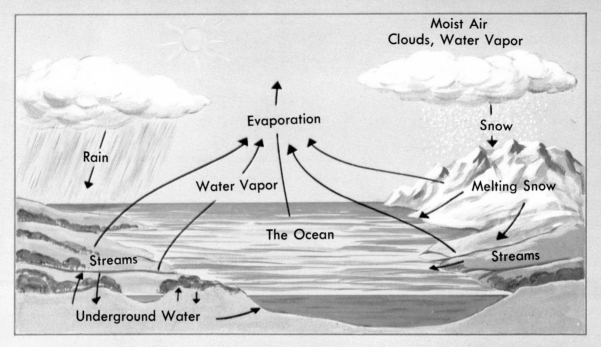

OBSERVE AND DISCUSS

This picture shows some of the travels of water. Study the picture carefully.

a. What happens to the water at the top of the ocean?

b. What happens to snow in warm weather? Where does the warmth come from? What may happen next?

c. What may happen to clouds when they become cool? When they become very cold? When they become warmer? What may warm the clouds?

d. A man digs and finds water underground. Where do you think it came from?

e. Plants get water from the soil. How does the water get into the soil? How does the water become underground water?

264

FIND OUT FROM OTHERS

1. Plan a trip to a place where a new house is being built. Find out about the water supply for the house. Prepare a list of questions to ask. Here are a few for you to begin with:

    a. What carries the water into the house?

    b. Where are the pipes that carry the water through the house?

    c. What are the pipes made of?

    d. Is there a water meter? If so, what is it used for?

    e. How can the water be shut off when the pipes need to be fixed?

    f. How is dirty water carried away from the house?

2. Plan a class trip to find out about your town water supply. Here are a few questions to ask:

    a. Where is the water stored?

    b. Does the water have to be purified? If so, how is it done?

    c. How does the water come to your town?

    d. What are some things you can do to help save water?

3. Find out how people who live in the country get their drinking water.

265

14

Cycle of a Mineral

Here is a story without a beginning and without an end. It is the story of a mineral called lime.

But a story has to begin somewhere. It could begin with a blade of grass or with a cup of milk. It could take place at the bottom of the sea, on top of a mountain, or inside this beautiful limestone cave.

Somewhere in the story a fish comes in—and a farmer—and you!

So you begin the story. Get some lime that looks like water. Change it into lime that looks like stone.

Turn the page and find out how to do this.

EXPERIMENT

You will need a glass of limewater and a soda straw.

Limewater is lime dissolved in water. You can buy limewater at the drugstore. It is quite cheap and cannot hurt you even if you drink it. The limewater is clear and has no color, like drinking water.

Blow gently into the limewater through a drinking straw. Keep blowing gently until the limewater stops getting milky.

Let the limewater stand for a while. Soon you will see tiny white grains sink to the bottom.

Pour off the water. Let the tiny grains dry.

In your breath is a gas called carbon dioxide. The limewater and carbon dioxide formed the white grains. These grains are made of the same substances as the limestone in seashells.

Sea Animals Build Shells

Sea animals have almost the same things that you used in your experiment. They build their stonelike houses in almost the same way. All around the animals is seawater with lime dissolved in it. Inside them is carbon dioxide. This is the same substance that you blew out in your breath.

The carbon dioxide and the lime come together inside the animals and form their limestone shells. Bit by bit, as the animal grows bigger, its shell house grows bigger, too.

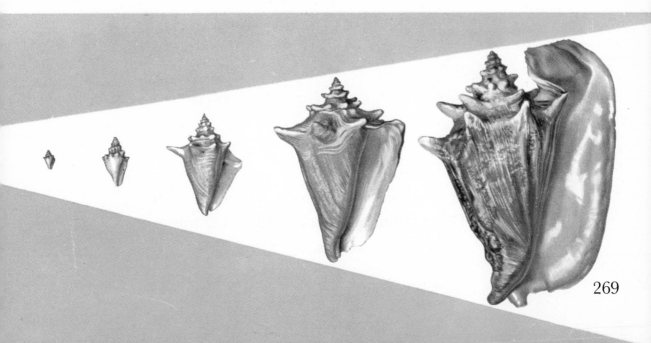

269

Volute

Atlantic Bay Scallop

Calico Scallop

New England Neptune

Lettered Olive

Common Nutmeg

Eastern Paper Bubble

Common Atlantic Vase

Common Jingle Shells

Dove Shell

Barbados
Keyhole Limpet

Atlantic
Margin Shell

Atlantic Ribbed Mussel

Littleneck
Clam

Atlantic
Shark Eye

Conch

Quahog

270 **Shells of the East Coast**

California
Cone

Western Murex

Pacific Oyster

California Bubble

Tegula

Great Keyhole Limpet

West Coast Moon Shell

Oregon Triton

Rosy Jackknife Clam

Pacific Cockleshell

Periwinkle

Tusk Shell

Common Pacific Littleneck

Blue Mussel

Pismo Clam

Red Abalone

California Hornshell

Shells of the West Coast

271

You Make Limestone

Sea animals are wonderful! But you are wonderful, too. You, too, build something made of minerals almost like limestone. Your bones and teeth! Right now, this very minute, your body is making this material and is building bones and teeth with it.

Bones and teeth contain a mineral called **calcium.** Lime, limestone, and seashells also contain calcium.

You get calcium from the food you eat and drink. Many kinds of plant and animal foods have calcium in them. Milk has the most. It is very good for people whose bones and teeth are still growing.

Calcium and Other Minerals

There is calcium in milk, and milk comes from cows. How do cows get calcium? They get it from plants they eat. Where do the plants get it?

There is dissolved calcium in the soil. Some of it soaks down into the ground and joins water underground. Some calcium soaks into the roots of plants.

What happens to minerals that the plants take in through their roots?

When we eat the plant, or when we drink the milk from the cow that ate the plant, we get calcium and other minerals. Every time a plant is pulled up by a farmer, minerals are taken away. Every time a cow bites off a blade of grass, minerals are taken away. Then there are fewer minerals in the soil.

The picture on this page shows what happened to spinach plants that were grown in soil with very little calcium.

How would you plan an experiment to find out whether plants grow better in soil with some calcium?

Limestone Underground

Some limestone dissolves down into the soil. But not all of it is carried away in underground water. In the picture you can see where some of it went.

Deep underground, in many parts of the world, there are strange and beautiful caves. Huge stone pillars seem to grow from the floor to the roof. Huge spears of stone, like giant icicles, hang from the roof. The entire cave, with its pillars and spears, was made by water and air!

Long ago there was solid, hard limestone here. A brook flowed through this rock. As it splashed along, air dissolved into the water.

As the carbon dioxide from the air dissolves into the water, it forms a substance that can cause limestone to dissolve. As the water flows in the limestone, this substance seeps slowly into the cracks and dissolves the limestone.

Here is a way of seeing it happen more quickly.

EXPERIMENT

You will need some clear vinegar, a few bits of seashells, and a glass.

Put the bits of shell into the glass. Pour some vinegar over them. What do you observe?

As the vinegar bubbles and fizzes, it is dissolving the limestone in the shells.

Leave your shells in the vinegar for a few hours. Pour off the vinegar. Scratch the shells with your fingernail. What happens?

The substance formed by carbon dioxide and water dissolves limestone in the same way that vinegar dissolves limestone, but more slowly. Thousands and thousands of years go by while the water with the carbon dioxide in it dissolves more and more limestone, forming a bigger and bigger cave.

Putting Minerals Back

Some minerals go underground with water. Some go into plants. If a farmer keeps taking away plants from the soil and does not put anything back, the soil becomes poor. It does not have enough minerals for the plants growing in it.

But good farmers do not let the soil become poor. They put minerals back into the soil. The farmers do this by spreading minerals over the soil. Rainwater dissolves the minerals and carries them down into the soil. Then the soil has minerals for growing plants.

Where do we get the minerals to put back into the soil? Let's see where we get one mineral, calcium.

Limestone contains large amounts of calcium. Machines dig the limestone out of mountains. Other machines crush it. Then it is heated. It becomes a white powder called lime. When the lime is spread on soil, it is slowly dissolved.

You can see this for yourself.

Problem

1. Get a little powdered lime in a farm-supply place or paint store. Spread the lime on some soil and sprinkle water on it. What happens?

2. Find out why you can get lime in a paint store.

3. Find a building made with limestone. Examine the face of the stone with a magnifying lens. What do you observe?

277

Calcium Journey

1. The calcium journey goes on forever. Mountains are slowly worn away by wind and water. Heat and cold slowly crack the stones. Men break them apart. Over millions of years, huge limestone mountains are broken into pieces and dissolved.

2. Dissolved limestone soaks into soil, into plants, into underground streams, into rivers. Water carries it away. Rivers flow to the sea.

3. From seawater it goes into seashells and bones. These pile up in the sea, layer upon layer. They become pressed together. They form limestone.

278

4. Later the land may rise above the sea. The layers of limestone become mountains of limestone again. Water will carry the calcium to the sea again. Other sea animals will use the calcium for making shells and bones.

Over and over again the things of the earth are used, and changed as they are used, and used again and again. Nothing is lost.

READABILITY

Science Far and Near, the third-grade book of the Heath Science Series, meets the requirements of third-grade readability. The Spache Readability Formula reveals that this book has a grade level of 3.1.

Within this readability framework, correct science words are introduced to ensure proper understanding of the content. The new science words are introduced and clarified through both text and illustrations.

Words assumed to be known in *Science Far and Near* are words which appear in the Heath word list. This is a list of words common to 5 out of 8 of the most widely used basal readers at the second-grade level and below, and 8 out of 8 of these basal readers at the third-grade level. Also assumed to be known are the words which appear in *A Reading Vocabulary for the Primary Grades* by Arthur I. Gates.

There are 374 words assumed to be new in *Science Far and Near.* These words are listed below in the order of their appearance in the text. Words which are scientific terms or are used for the interpretation of science information are in italics.

1	*chest*	25 *prairie*	41
2 *cereal*	13 *muscles*	26 poke	42 *balance*
vibration	*exhale*	27	snipping
3 pluck	*inhale*	28 *lizards*	dip
larynx	14	29 *watermelon*	43 *dragonfly*
4 *jet*	15 steady	crumpled	44 *wriggler*
plane	zip	30 *cactus*	*pupa*
tube	*million*	result	45 depend
5 *substance*	cause	probably	*oxygen*
plastic	study	*evaporate*	*carbon dioxide*
6 *sponge*	16 aid	useful	46 *gills*
7 instant	17 *dolphins*	31 *spine*	*test*
problem	earphone	special	47
thunder	18 repair	32 supply	48 *beaver*
lightning	*muffler*	shelter	49 slaps
flashed	*depths*	pretend	50 heaped
8 important	19 hose	*geranium*	51
underneath	guitar	33 neighborhood	52 *beetle*
9 *nerves*	carton	34	*grub*
brain	possible	35 *surface*	53 crumble
distance	thumbtack	*community*	*fungi*
10 closer	20	36	*fungus*
explain	21	37	*mold*
11 *stethoscope*	22	38	54 slice
directions	23 *scales*	39	fuzzy
12 *pumps*	24	40 shown	*growths*

knobs
spores
55
56 *bacteria*
57 *aquarium*
58 *pebble*
59 *snail*
tip
sinks
60 *cycle*
jelly
guppies
fin
mouthful
61
62 *algae*
fasten
63
64 bulletin
65 container
arrange
66
67
68
69 flattened
70 *dissolve*
71 *teaspoonful*
trickle
72 seep
usually
73
74 Utah
75
76 shallow
77 discover
copper
scoop
vacuum
78 *valleys*
deal
instruments
oceanographers
79 drift
80
81 *oysters*
ragged
scallops
lobster
clicked

squids
octopuses
shrimps
82
83 fisherman
salmon
84
85 fifteen
spout
86 valuable
blubber
towed
margarine
vitamins
liver
fertilizer
perfume
87
88 *cucumbers*
razor
cling
billions
89 *pitch*
endless
lit
growing
90 Columbia River
91
92
93 single
tomato
doesn't
94 supermarket
pinch
95 bare
96 clump
rinse
separate
fern
97
98
99 *sprout*
firm
101 *moist*
102
103 formed
fibers
growth
104

105 syrup
sap
liquid
drilled
drips
106 delicious
hardness
steel
107 sample
108
109
110
111
112 according
scattered
113 daily
114
115 *invented*
benefit
applied
116 *pattern*
twist
117 *pigments*
118 *biologists*
improving
diseases
cure
119
120 *cocoon*
silk
moth
121 China
unwound
Pasteur
122 *celery*
split
examine
apart
123
124 *ripens*
petals
pod
base
'fluffy
cotton gin
spool
125
126 *weaving*
looms

spun
burlap
tend
127 *automated*
128 *dyes*
soak
spinach
beets
unwashed
129 *chemists*
fade
130 *rayon*
hardened
vinegar
131 *woven*
label
group
slot
bent
list
132
133
134 *modeling*
polish
peel
thickness
135 *elastic*
untwist
knitting
yarn
136
137
138 *insulator*
insulation
139
140 *refrigerators*
141 whether
142 *rays*
143 *reflected*
144 *fuel*
145 *pint*
146
147 *safety*
furnace
148 *steam*
149 *radiators*
chalkboard
erasers
150

282